Praise for

The Client-Centered Law Firm

"For more than a decade, Jack Newton has had the unenviable job of selling software to lawyers. With remarkable success, he has prevailed and, on the way, built a deep understanding of what makes law firms tick and stumble. This book is an excellent distillation of this insight, above all calling for law firms to swing round and face the market, to focus relentlessly on the needs of clients, and to ceaselessly improve client experiences. A considerable and important contribution to the law firm literature."

PROFESSOR RICHARD SUSSKIND OBE, AUTHOR OF *TOMORROW'S LAWYERS*

"We as lawyers often focus on 'what' legal services we provide instead of on 'how' we do it. Jack Newton's new book, *The Client-Centered Law Firm*, is (rightly) all about the 'how.' Based on Jack's wealth of experience servicing clients in the legal marketplace, this book provides a useful guide on how to enhance client service with client-centricity and also, importantly, how to measure progress. It is a must-read for all types of legal professionals."

MICHELE DESTEFANO, PROFESSOR OF LAW, UNIVERSITY OF MIAMI, AFFILIATED FACULTY, HARVARD LAW SCHOOL EXECUTIVE EDUCATION, FOUNDER, LAWWITHOUTWALLS

"In the age of Amazon and Uber, the lesson for law firms is that experience matters—not just legal experience, but also the experience you provide your clients. Drawing on his own experience as founder and CEO of one of the legal industry's most-successful companies, Jack Newton provides a practical blueprint for building a client-centered law firm, making the case for why it matters through data and examples, and then guiding you through the process of redesigning your own firm and measuring success."

BOB AMBROGI, PUBLISHER AND EDITOR-IN-CHIEF, LAWSITESBLOG.COM AND LEXBLOG.COM

"Jack Newton understands the legal system was designed by the people working in it—rather than those using it. Newton knows we have to make the system better by putting our users first. He delivers, with unequaled passion, drive, and knowledge, an inspiring call to action, a roadmap for success, and a platform for change—all of which will benefit the consumers of legal services and the lawyers serving them. I loved Jack's book, and you will too."

KEVIN O'KEEFE, CEO AND FOUNDER, LEXBLOG, INC.

"How do you balance the success of your firm with the needs of your clients? This is the dilemma with which many law firms struggle. Jack Newton removes this conflict in *The Client-Centered Law Firm* by showing how focusing on the client's experience as well as their outcomes helps them and the law firm succeed. If you want guidance navigating the law firm / client divide, this book is for you."

JOSHUA LENON, LAWYER IN RESIDENCE, CLIO, BOARD MEMBER, LEXUM

"This is quite possibly the most important book of the decade for lawyers. While most legal books are one or the other, *The Client-Centered Law Firm* expertly balances inspiring philosophy with tangible guidance in a way that only someone with Jack Newton's understanding of the legal industry could do."

JORDAN L. COUCH, PARTNER, PALACE LAW

"The legal industry is changing and it's time to break free of the traditional law model. Jack Newton provides the reasoning and the pathway to develop a client-centered mindset and change the legal industry—for good."

KIMBERLY Y. BENNETT, ATTORNEY AND FOUNDER, K BENNETT LAW LLC

"If terms like 'flywheel,' 'design thinking,' 'client-centered,' 'journey mapping,' and 'data-driven law' are words that do not describe your law firm, then this book will not only revolutionize the way you visualize the practice of law, it will also help you transform your outdated systems, retool your practice to thrive in the new legal economy and, best of all, return you to the days of doing what you love and loving what you do."

PATRICK PALACE, MANAGING PARTNER, PALACE LAW

"Law firms are businesses. In *The Client-Centered Law Firm*, Jack Newton applies the lessons he used to build Clio into one of legal tech's biggest success stories—such as empathy, attentiveness, and creating effortless experiences—to help law firms achieve better product-market fit with their clients. With metrics, case studies, and practical advice, this is the playbook for running a successful law firm."

ED WALTERS, CEO, FASTCASE

"If you're looking to ramp up your law firm then *The Client-Centered Law Firm* has you covered. Filled with insights from industry-leader Jack Newton and real-world examples, this book is the ultimate guide for lawyers looking for a competitive edge."

JANINE SICKMEYER, MANAGING DIRECTOR AND FOUNDER, NEXTCHAPTER

"*The Client-Centered Law Firm* brings the entrepreneurial perspective much needed in today's market for legal services. Jack nails a vision for the future of law in the 21st century with insightful commentary and relatable business insights. This book is a must-read."

ANDREW ARRUDA, CO-FOUNDER/CEO, ROSS INTELLIGENCE

"Just as Clio, the multimillion-dollar business that Jack Newton has built, has steadily moved so much of the legal sector into the modern era, *The Client-Centered Law Firm* is a Trojan horse of radically transformative ideas for the legal sector. Newton has much to share with legal professionals about building a law practice in the modern economy. Smart legal professionals will find themselves, just as I found myself, hanging on every word and eager for what Newton will share next."

DAN LEAR, CHIEF INSTIGATOR, RIGHT BRAIN LAW

"A compelling case as to why lawyers have to embrace technology in order to survive, presented by someone who knows more about the intersection of law and technology than almost anybody else. If this was a case in a courtroom, the opposing side would be hard-pressed to find a lawyer."

CHRISTOPH JANZ, PARTNER, POINT NINE CAPITAL

"Jack Newton, the CEO and Co-founder of Clio, cares deeply about how to elevate the practice of law through technology. In his new book, *The Client-Centered Law Firm*, Jack lays out a blueprint for how law firms can succeed in a world that is increasingly driven by experiences. A must read for every forward-thinking lawyer!"

BORIS WERTZ, FOUNDER AND GENERAL PARTNER, VERSION ONE VENTURES

"Every lawyer who wants to take their game to the next level needs to read this book. For solos to global firms, what Jack presents here is the beginning roadmap for designing competitive advantage in a manner that accentuates the opportunities for taking action and the risks for not. If your competitor reads this book before you, I would worry."

JOSH KUBICKI, CO-FOUNDER, BOLD DUCK STUDIO

"This book really has it all: deep industry reflection, insights on how lawyers actually run their firms, customer strategy, organizational philosophy, and meaningful tips for lawyers on improving their lives and practices all along the way. Jack has built one of the most successful businesses in legal—ever—and this book should be a great tool for anyone hoping to build one too."

MARK BRITTON, CEO, FOUNDER, AND FORMER CHAIRMAN, AVVO

THE
**CLIENT
CENTERED**
LAW FIRM

THE CLIENT CENTERED LAW FIRM

How to Succeed in an Experience-Driven World

JACK NEWTON

Foreword by JORDAN FURLONG

BLUE CHECK
PUBLISHING

ISBN 978-1-989603-32-1 (paperback/hardcover)
ISBN 978-1-7770097-0-0 (ebook)

Blue Check Publishing
Produced by Page Two
www.pagetwo.com

Cover design by Jennifer Lum & Danielle Giroux
Cover illustration by Isla Newton
Interior design by Jennifer Lum & Justin Chow

clientcenteredlawfirm.com

To Tonia, Ian, Patrick, and Isla.
Thank you for your support and encouragement
over the last decade—I couldn't have done it without you.

CONTENTS

PART 3

FOREWORD

I'VE RECENTLY RETURNED from a trip to a parallel universe, where an alternative timeline of history has unfolded. It was a fascinating place, and I want to share with you some of what I saw there.

I saw the enormously profitable entertainment giant Blockbuster, which watched the internet develop and understood its potential as a movie distribution engine. Blockbuster used its vast collection of films and its data about customers' buying habits to become the world's leading source of movies online, and now even produces its own films. "We're not in the business of renting videocassettes," Blockbuster's leaders told themselves. "We're in the business of helping people enjoy the movie they want to see tonight."

I saw the great photography multinational Kodak, whose researchers were among the first to develop the technology behind digital cameras—but rather than dismissing their work, Kodak's leaders saw an opportunity to develop an entirely new line of products. The company eventually invented digital photo technology that it licenses to Microsoft's popular "mPhone" at an enormous profit. "We're not in the business of selling film," Kodak's leaders realized. "We're in the business of helping people take pictures."

And I saw the most powerful and valuable company in the

world: Sears, the global online shopping colossus. Leveraging its long history as a source of convenient purchasing—from its catalogues to its distribution centers—Sears understood that the internet was the most convenient possible way for people to shop, and it invested heavily and successfully in the technology to make it happen. "We're not in the business of running department stores," Sears's leaders said. "We're in the business of helping people easily get the products and services they need."

In our own universe, of course, things didn't turn out quite this way. These longstanding market incumbents missed the opportunity presented by new technology to rethink just what business they were really in, and to re-design their companies in ways that could enable them to use this technology for greater growth and higher profits.

But this alternative timeline reminds us that established market leaders need not inevitably lose out to upstarts and challengers from the outside. Not only is it *possible* for incumbents to reap the rewards of technological changes, it is incumbents who are *best positioned* to do so. They already have the market dominance, the financial reserves, the brand power, and the proven track record of success. All they need is to be willing to think a little differently about themselves and about their customers' actual needs.

This is exactly where the legal profession finds itself as we open the third decade of the 21st century. It is now beyond all doubt that technology has changed and will continue to change the conditions under which legal services are bought and sold. There is no going back to the way things used to be. And we shouldn't *want* to go back, because we can now serve our clients better and faster and less expensively and with a higher degree of quality than we could before. We're at the dawn of a golden age of legal services.

Lawyers can lead the way into that new age—if we are willing, if we have the courage and the foresight, to understand that technology and change and upheaval are not threats, they're *opportunities*. Opportunities for us to give more help and better advice to more people and more businesses, faster and more profitably than in the past. Opportunities to work fewer hours, connect more deeply with clients, run better legal businesses, and lead happier personal lives.

Are you in the business of billing hours? Are you in the business of filling out forms and signing documents and attending meetings? Are you in the business of measuring out your life in six-minute increments?

If you are the lawyer I think you are, then the answer is no. You are in the business of helping people solve problems, of putting lives back on track, of helping businesses grow and prosper. But it's possible that your own law business has started to chase and measure and reward the wrong things— that it has forgotten its intended purpose, what and who it's actually for.

The purpose of your law business is your clients.

The future of law is client-centered. Jack Newton understands this fundamental truth as well as anyone, and the book you're holding is an essential and engaging how-to guide for building an outstanding legal business in this new legal market. Clear and compelling, filled with real-life examples from both the legal and corporate worlds, this book will show you how to value the client experience, map your clients' journeys, and infuse your firm's culture with empathy and collaboration.

Jack's most important message to lawyers, which you'll

find throughout the book, is this: The time to act is now. He's right. Today, you're standing at the same fork in the road where Blockbuster, Kodak, and Sears once stood. But you don't have to follow their examples. You can make a different and better choice than they did.

It's time to develop a client-centered law practice. It's time to rethink and redesign your law business. It's time to write your own alternative history.

JORDAN FURLONG
Legal Market Analyst and Principal, Law21

THE CLIENT-CENTERED REVOLUTION

FOR MORE THAN 10 years, my goal has been to empower lawyers to spend more time and energy on what they love: practicing law. I've spent many hours talking to lawyers, legal professionals, regulators, consultants, and IT professionals about what law firms need to succeed. I've also been lucky enough to witness massive change in the legal industry, with firms migrating to the cloud and becoming more data-driven.

But change isn't coming fast enough. Throughout the years, one nagging theme has stood out to me: Most lawyers and law firms don't prioritize *product-market fit* between their services and their clients. Some do, and countless leading legal thinkers have been talking about it for years, but the vast majority don't think about how their overall services match client needs. The opportunity for the legal industry to not only survive but to thrive hinges on our ability to strengthen the product-market fit between lawyers and consumers of legal services.

Product-market fit is the degree to which your product or service satisfies market demand. In the tech industry, if you don't have it, you don't survive, period. Finding product-market fit isn't simple or straightforward. If it were, then we wouldn't see 90% of startups failing.

Companies like Uber, Netflix, and Airbnb have radically raised the baseline of user ease that customers now expect thanks to rapid ride-hailing, instant access to movies, and luxurious, affordable short-term vacation rentals that are available anywhere in the world. This new baseline has influenced what today's legal client expects from their lawyer. But, unfortunately, law firms aren't yet delivering.

According to the *2018 Legal Trends Report*, many legal clients (40%) experience frustration when hiring a lawyer, and many more aren't using lawyers for their legal needs: 57% of consumers surveyed for the report have had a life issue that could have been handled legally but wasn't. A report from the World Justice Project found that 77% of people in the US didn't get legal help for their legal issues in 2018. This product-market gap in legal is causing potential clients to simply not use lawyers.

I believe it's possible to bridge this gap and for the legal industry to succeed, but it's going to require accepting that the status quo is no longer working and committing to long-term change. I also believe there's an approach that can get us there—and that's what this book is about.

The future for law firms is client-centered.

Client-centered law firms succeed because they compete on experience in a world where experience is king. This focus leads them to better reviews, more referrals, and more returning clients, and it doesn't come at the expense of their internal operations—far from it. Client-centered firms know that providing a good client experience and running an efficient, profitable law firm aren't opposing ideas. With the right approach, they drive each other.

There's plenty of opportunity for law firms that are willing to take charge of their futures: A few years ago, Thomson Reuters reported that the US legal services market was worth $437 billion annually, and that's just the tip of the iceberg. As we'll explore, there's a tremendous amount of latent demand in the legal market that both alternative legal service providers *and* law firms can access, provided that law firms focus on delivering a better product-market fit. Finding that fit starts with a better client experience.

This book is both a rallying call for a tectonic shift in the legal industry and a handbook for becoming a client-centered law firm. It's divided into three parts, covering the what, why, and how of running a client-centered practice, and it features numerous examples from forward-thinking legal professionals who are already putting client-centered practices into action.

Part 1 discusses why the legal market is changing and why a client-centered approach makes sense in today's experience-driven world. I challenge the idea that lawyers are different from other service providers, especially in the eyes of the consumer, and explain why I believe that we're now at an inflection point, driven by changing consumer demands. I talk about how expectations have shifted for today's legal clients, how a lack of product-market fit has led to immense latent demand for legal services, how a client-*centered* approach differs from a client-*first* one, and how a client-centered approach empowers your firm to harness something called the flywheel effect to grow and thrive. I also go into detail about why the client experience you provide is seen as part and parcel of the product clients are paying you for—right alongside your legal advice or any legal deliverables—which means that providing a good client experience is a necessity rather than a nice-to-have.

Part 2 covers what it means to run a client-centered law firm, including five core values, and how to cultivate a client-centered mindset. I talk about client-journey mapping—a tool that visualizes the different stages of a client's experience with your law firm to identify opportunities for improvement—and explain why developing deep empathy (and acting on it) is critical for client-centered firms.

Part 3 is your toolkit for implementing lasting client-centered change at your law firm. It explains how to effectively design processes and tools, how to get buy-in for change from staff and lawyers, and how to navigate the shift to a client-centered culture. I end off with advice on how to measure success, as well as how to act on feedback and data insights: This final step keeps the flywheel of success turning, enabling you to increase internal efficiencies, grow your client base, and thrive like never before.

One note on semantics. Design thinking fans will note that there's a subtle difference between creating good client experiences and *designing for* good client experiences. Technically, you can't create an experience *for* anyone else, because you can't control how anyone else thinks or feels. Also, the experiences that drive people to seek legal help stretch far beyond the interactions they might have with a law firm, and it's impossible to control all external factors. You can create a bright, welcoming lobby and make the client-intake process as painless as possible, but if you practice family law, many clients will still be facing one of the most difficult challenges of their lives, and a bright setting won't take that pain away. It *does* however create the scaffolding needed to make your client's experience as effortless and positive as possible—in other words, you've designed *for* a better experience. To keep things simple, I refer to this idea as creating good/better client experiences throughout the book.

The world is constantly changing, and law firms, like every other type of business, must adapt. Whether you're a partner, an associate, an IT manager, a paralegal, or a legal assistant; whether you're a consultant or an office manager; whether you're a solo lawyer, a student, or a member of a large law firm—I hope this book sparks a meaningful shift for you and inspires you to pass that client-centered spark on to others as well.

Most of all, I hope that you turn inspiration into action and that your law firm succeeds like never before in today's experience-driven world.

PART 1

1

THE AGE OF EXPERIENCE

FOR TODAY'S CONSUMER, experience is everything.

The myriad tiny interactions that happen before, during, and after a consumer buys a product might seem inconsequential individually, but collectively they can make or break a business. This is true whether your organization sells a tangible product or provides a service.

Think about how you feel when you enter a Starbucks. You enter a warmly lit, cleanly designed coffee shop with plenty of space to sit. You order your beverage of choice from the barista, personalized to your taste (that is, if you haven't ordered using the app ahead of time). There's free Wi-Fi in case you need to check your email while you wait, which is good news, because while you'd love to stop and enjoy the coffee, you're having an incredibly busy day as always. You receive your order promptly and you're on your way.

Now think about how it feels to order something from Amazon. You haven't traveled in a while, and you're about to go on a trip, but when you get your old carry-on suitcase out of your closet, you discover that one of the wheels has fallen off and your zipper has broken. You need a new one, but you don't want something that's going to fall apart again. You want a quality piece, reasonably priced. You head to Amazon. com. A quick search brings up a number of options. Detailed descriptions and reviews give you an idea of which product best meets your needs, and once you've made your choice, you place your order with a single click. You select one day shipping—your purchase arrives at your doorstep the next day, just in time to pack—and you head off on your trip without issue.

In both of these scenarios, you got what you wanted, and you got it quickly and easily in a way that made sense to you. You didn't get value solely from the product you were buying; you got value from your *experience* buying the product as well.

The customer (or client) experience is the totality of a person's interactions with any given business. It's a key piece of the value that organizations offer. Modern consumers expect more than a product or service: they expect an end-to-end customer experience that makes sense. When the customer experience is negative, or even lukewarm, that's detrimental to the value a company provides. Good service is a baseline expectation, and customers won't put up with less. They'll take their business elsewhere.

Consider this scenario: you decide to buy your carry-on luggage directly from a brand's website instead of via Amazon. You need information to choose the suitcase best for you, but the website takes forever to load. You try contacting the company with a question, but the phone number is hard to find, and no one answers your call. You fill out the "contact us" form, but there's no confirmation when you click "submit," and you never get a response. Not only will you likely not make that purchase, you might complain to your friends and you certainly won't recommend or revisit that supplier. Or even buy that brand on Amazon.

Joshua Kubicki, cofounder of Bold Duck Studio and former head of strategy at Seyfarth Shaw, often speaks about how a focus on experience transformed Starbucks from a humble commodity supplier—of coffee—into something much more valuable. The experience at Starbucks (well-designed shops, excellent service, streamlined ordering, and more) is the bedrock of a brand that's grown from a small Seattle coffee shop to a global business with a market capitalization of nearly $90 billion. Starbucks is the world's largest coffee chain with 27,000 locations in more than 76 countries worldwide.

Law firms aren't coffee shops, but there's a useful parallel: Law firms deliver a product (i.e., legal advice) and an experience (i.e., interactions with your law firm), and clients view these as one and the same. This is true whether your firm serves individuals or large businesses; at the end of the day, we're all human.

This quote from an interview with Joshua best explains the point:

> Lawyers think of client value as the advice and counsel they're giving, or their work product, which is absolutely, hands down, one of the things that clients buy. But that's not the *only* thing clients are buying. If you are a pain to do business with, or you're just rude, or you're obnoxious, or you can't get a bill out on time, or your bills don't make any sense, sooner or later that client relationship is going to erode. You're providing negative value even though you may be the smartest lawyer there is.

It doesn't take much for clients to look elsewhere for better service. According to the results of the PwC's Future of Customer Experience survey, **32% of customers would stop doing business with a brand they loved after just one bad experience.**

A good experience, on the other hand, is the difference that makes someone choose one coffee shop, online retailer—or law firm—over another. And since law is an industry based on reputation and word-of-mouth referrals, experience is crucial and can't be overlooked.

Expectation Osmosis

A cross-industry trend that's important to take a look at here—because it affects the legal industry in a big way—is how consumer choice has exploded. Consider how, in the recent past, people had few choices if they wanted to watch a movie, book a place to stay on vacation, or get a ride from point A to point B. The options available came with mildly inconvenient experiences—not unpleasant, just less than ideal—and people accepted that. They drove to Blockbuster. They wandered through aisles of DVDs and VHS tapes wondering what to rent, because the hot new release was taken already. They forgot to return the tape on time and were charged late fees. They paid handsomely for hotels in business districts far from the cultural centers of the cities they visited and booked rooms without any idea of what they'd look like. They got soaked in the rain while trying to hail a taxi, accepted whatever price the meter landed on at the end of the trip, and fumbled for cash when the credit card machine broke—again.

In 1997, Netflix gave consumers the option to rent DVDs by mail, eliminating the drive to the video rental store. Then the company offered the option to pay a flat monthly fee to stream as many movies and television shows from their collection as you'd like—with no need to rent individual titles and no late fees. They even developed a personalized recommendation system to make it easy to find something you might like to watch. Today, with over 150 million subscribers globally and a market capitalization of more than $115 billion, Netflix is one of the largest video-streaming services in the world. Blockbuster is bankrupt.

In 2008, two roommates and a friend launched airbedandbreakfast.com to rent out air mattresses and provide breakfast to guests so that they could afford their rent. This morphed into Airbnb, providing site visitors with extensive photos, reviews, and clear pricing for thousands of rental accommodations. There are now more than 6 million Airbnb listings worldwide and at least 2 million people stay in an Airbnb rental every night.

In 2010, UberCab launched, giving people the ability to hail a luxury black car for a ride with the click of a button. No more waiting in the rain. In 2012, Uber launched UberX as a more affordable ride-hailing option, and today riders use the app and enjoy an up-front quoted price for their trip, automatic payment, and the ability to rate the driver. Uber is now available in 700 cities across the globe and has an estimated 110 million users worldwide; 14 million Uber trips are taken every day. But Uber wasn't the only company to see the value of providing a better ride: Lyft launched in 2012 as a service of Zimride, a carpooling company launched in 2007, and the ridesharing industry has exploded around the world.

In each of these cases, customers are still getting the same product or service as before, but the *experience* is completely different. Finding a movie to watch, a place to stay, or a ride across town no longer comes with a slightly annoying experience. People have a choice, and when the choice is between a subpar experience and an effortless one, they vote with their dollars and choose the latter.

Companies like Netflix, Airbnb, and Uber aren't only changing expectations in their respective industries. They're changing expectations in *all* industries: If you're used to seeing exactly what you'd get and what you'd pay up-front when booking a vacation rental, why would you expect any less when working with a law firm?

Expectations have been set in arenas that are relatively inconsequential, like watching a movie or hailing a ride. But when clients are going through a substantially difficult life event—like a civil lawsuit or divorce—they *need* that experience to be as painless as possible, and they now expect law firms to anticipate their needs. Consciously or unconsciously, your clients are comparing their experience with your firm to the five-star experiences they have elsewhere—and it's time for your firm to catch up.

If you don't like to think of your practice as a business, consider this: I'm not asking you to become a business mogul and focus on profits over the practice of law—I'm asking you to educate yourself on how to efficiently provide good client experiences and make strategic decisions about how you run your practice, so that you can spend more time practicing law.

Meeting Versus Exceeding Expectations

Today's consumer (who is also your legal client) has high expectations—but that may not mean what you think it does.

There's no need to dazzle and delight your clients at every opportunity. In fact, there's no need to *exceed* expectations at all. As long as you can *meet* expectations, you're good—and you'll be ahead of most law firms. The problem is this can be surprisingly hard to do.

In *The Effortless Experience*, Matthew Dixon, Nick Toman, and Rick DeLisi surveyed over 97,000 customers to ask about a recent service interaction they had and to see how this impacted customer loyalty. The findings were incredibly interesting. First, exceeding customer expectations made basically zero difference in how loyal a customer was likely to be (i.e., whether they'd continue paying for a given service or for products from the company). Loyalty plateaus once a customer's expectations are met.

A strategy of going above and beyond to create happy customers for life sounds good, but in reality, for most organizations, it's expensive and distracts from the core focus of a business. When you go the extra mile for one customer, that only impacts that one customer. Your grand gesture won't likely have a long-lasting effect on your day-to-day business. However, if you can improve your processes to help one client, you'll improve the experience for *all* of your clients. Taking care to ensure your clients' needs are met in the best possible way is a much better investment. It's also rare that opportunities to delight customers present themselves, and it's difficult to get it right. Providing a pleasant surprise for a customer in the form of free shipping is one thing, but providing a personalized surprise that deeply resonates with someone is difficult, even if you know them well.

What *does* make a difference in customer loyalty is how much *effort* a customer has to put in to resolve a given issue.

66 ——

If you can improve

your processes

to help one client,

you'll improve the

experience for all

of your clients.

—— 99

Four of the five biggest drivers of disloyalty resulting from customer service interactions were effort related. The biggest offender? Having to contact a company more than once to resolve an issue. That isn't surprising: No one likes calling their wireless carrier even once.

With that in mind, it's not hard to see why Netflix disrupted Blockbuster, why Airbnb disrupted the hotel industry, or why Uber disrupted the taxi industry. They didn't concern themselves with dazzling customers—they focused intently on giving them what they wanted in a more convenient way.

I've always had simple, predictable experiences with Uber and other ridesharing services. I usually get a pretty clean car. It's comfortable. The drivers are polite. They drive safely. And I can always get a ride when I need one. Contrast that with the taxi industry in Vancouver. At the time of writing, ridesharing has yet to come to the city, which means we still use good old-fashioned taxis to get from A to B. When I return from a business trip, I wait in line for up to 45 minutes outside the airport for a ride home. If I'm out late in downtown Vancouver, I'm rolling the dice as to whether a taxi will be willing to drive me all the way home (it's common for taxis to refuse service to riders wanting to go too far outside of the downtown core late at night).

This is the very embodiment of a fungible commodity differentiated by service. One version of a ride home is delivered with proper tools and technology to create an effortless experience, and the other is delivered without those things in a way that makes the experience negative. And that makes all the difference. In any city where Uber or other ridesharing services *are* available, I choose one of those over a taxi ride in a heartbeat—and many other consumers do too.

Most Uber drivers don't go out of their way to provide an amazing experience. Sure, there was that one time in New Orleans during our annual conference when our driver told us to "pick a song" from a tablet, kicking off a disco-ball light show and incredibly fun ride, but I don't use Uber expecting that every time. I use it because it meets my expectations for a quick and comfortable ride home. Who would wait 45 minutes for a taxi when they could order a ride in minutes with an app on their phone?

Unfortunately, the taxi industry has been slow to catch on to the need to better meet consumer expectations. That might be because in the past, they haven't had to: Many cities issue a limited number of medallions that must be displayed by taxis each year, so there's a cap on the number of cabs available at any given time. Taxis were once the only option (outside of public transit or private car services), so there was no need for the industry to consider the customer experience.

Understandably, taxi owners and drivers around the world who've paid exorbitant prices for taxi medallions are upset. Many have taken to the streets to protest ridesharing, arguing that it isn't fair for companies like Uber to circumvent the system. And one can certainly sympathize (to a point), but with the advent of Uber, the dynamic has shifted, and there's no going back. Customers have a simpler option for getting a ride, and they're voting with their dollars.

It's a similar story in legal: Some law firms still don't feel the pressure to provide a better client experience because they believe that as the only ones able to provide a certain product (in this case, legal advice), clients need them more than the other way around. As it did for the taxi industry, this adherence to the status quo in the legal industry is leading to a breaking point.

The legal profession is traditionally risk averse, and rightly so—but in this case, those who cling to the status quo are taking the biggest risk of all.

A Buyer's Market

For years, leading legal thinkers have been writing about how technology, the global economy, and innovative legal service providers are chipping away at the monopoly lawyers once held over the law. The legal industry is facing a crisis.

In his book *Law Is a Buyer's Market*, Jordan Furlong argues that while law was once a seller's market—with lawyers holding all the power and clients having no choice but to accept how firms operated—it is now a buyer's market, and clients are understandably sick of the old one-sided dynamic.

New technologies now do what only lawyers could once do, and these capabilities continue to grow. (Just think of Joshua Browder's DoNotPay bot: It's a chatbot created to help people fight parking tickets without needing to see a lawyer, and now you can also use it to sue.) The internet has given the public unprecedented access to legal knowledge. Globalization has led to the offshoring of legal services, with lowered pricing expectations. The global financial crisis took place over a decade ago, but we're still feeling the effects today. As Jordan points out, this means consumers are a hell of a lot more likely to avoid hiring a lawyer for their legal issues, and if they do hire one, they're more likely to want the bare minimum needed to solve their legal issue in order to keep costs down.

At the same time, regulations against the unauthorized practice of law have started to wane in states such as

"

Adherence to the status quo in the legal industry is leading to a breaking point.

"

Washington and New York, giving rise to partial "lawyer sub-
stitutes," or parallel technologies and providers that help with
bits and pieces of legal work. Needless to say, this stands to
further impact demand. (Jordan provides a nuanced discussion of the benefits and challenges of new providers of legal
services in his book, and I'd encourage you to read it.)

Some firms are already adapting to this new world. In her
book *Legal Upheaval*, Michele DeStefano talks about how
innovative law firms are using AI tools to help with tasks such
as document review, contract analysis, research, and even
litigation analytics. (Premonition is a tool that helps predict
which lawyers win which types of cases in front of particular
judges.) But in Michele's interviews with over 100 general
counsels (GCs) and law firm partners, the general consensus
was that firms have yet to catch up with other sectors in terms
of service and experience, and companies are getting frustrated. Sometimes, they want an in-depth legal solution, and
sometimes they want a quick and dirty one, and they expect
lawyers to respond to those needs. They also want lawyers to
anticipate knock-on effects and future problems and provide
solutions for those, and they want to know *what* to do with
their legal advice rather than being left to figure that out
themselves.

They don't want to have to call back twice. Sound familiar?

With changing market dynamics and a shift in demand
for the type of work people want from their lawyers, law
firms have a massive opportunity to differentiate themselves
based on experience. Technology can help with a lot, but it
can't do everything. The empathy, intuition, and special-
ized responses that come from real, live human experts are
things that only lawyers can offer. People and businesses

still want a sage guide to help them through whatever legal issue they're facing. If lawyers capitalize on this, they'll position themselves to ride the wave of changing economies and technologies and achieve huge success. But if they don't, they risk being left behind as the industry and client expectations evolve without them.

Experience Is King

Lawyers have an incredibly important job in upholding the laws that hold our society together. But their role reaches well beyond interpreting the law and providing legal advice: Lawyers guide people through their entire experience when facing a legal issue—from a client's first interaction with a law firm to the final invoice and any follow-up. Their service extends beyond legal deliverables, even beyond meeting rooms and phone calls. It encompasses every single interaction a client has with a firm.

But when it comes to providing thoughtful client service, many law firms are missing the mark. Clio's *2018 Legal Trends Report* analyzed aggregated and anonymized data from tens of thousands of legal professionals and surveyed 1,968 legal professionals and 1,336 consumers to take a closer look at the industry's trends. There were a few notable findings related to client experience.

First, consumers aren't happy with the level of service that the legal industry provides.

To get an overall read on how satisfied clients are with their experiences using lawyers, the researchers looked at factors that impacted Net Promoter Score (NPS), a metric commonly used to rate customer satisfaction. It's calculated based on answers to the question "On a scale of 0 to 10, how likely are you to recommend my services to a friend or colleague?" and graded on a scale of -100 to +100. (You will learn how to track your firm's NPS in Chapter 12.) The NPS for the legal industry as a whole was a low 25—on par with wireless carriers, banks, and credit card companies. For comparison, high NPS companies such as Amazon and Netflix—companies that you likely know and love in your day-to-day life and that put a serious focus on the customer experience—have scores closer to 70.

Second, law firms don't realize that their clients are less than enthused about their services: 40% of clients feel frustration as part of the experience when hiring a lawyer, but only 8% of law firms perceive this to be the case.

Third, lawyers don't communicate with clients in ways that their clients expect. The report compared how clients wanted to undertake certain interactions (updates, payments, and signing contracts via email, phone, or in person, etc.) with how lawyers *thought* clients wanted to undertake those interactions, and lawyers definitely didn't accurately predict what clients wanted. For example, 70% of clients want to tell their lawyer about the details of their matter in person, but only 3% of lawyers thought this was the case. Lawyers predicted that clients would prefer email (51%) or a phone call (39%).

Finally, a lot of consumers simply aren't using lawyers. Only 65% of people surveyed for the report had actually hired a lawyer despite having a legal problem they'd faced in the two years prior. Many consumers are concerned that hiring a lawyer is overwhelming (39%) or too much trouble (32%), which impacts their decision to get legal help. This lines up

"

_____

40% of clients feel frustration as part of the experience when hiring a lawyer, but only 8% of law firms perceive this to be the case.

_____

"

with a report from the World Justice Project: 77% of those surveyed in the United States didn't turn to an authority or third party to resolve their legal issue. In the United Kingdom, that number is a staggering 93%.

Meanwhile, lawyers aren't spending as much time as they'd like lawyering, in part because they're focused on trying to find new clients. The *2018 Legal Trends Report* found that lawyers are only spending about 2.4 hours per day on billable work, and since 75% of lawyers also report working outside of regular business hours, that's not much time spent practicing law. But on any given day, lawyers are also spending an average 1.4 hours networking to meet new clients and build referrals, and nearly an hour on tasks related to advertising. In Clio's 2017 report, lawyers surveyed said they spent on average 33% of their non-billable hours on business development, but 41% said that if they had even more time, they'd spend that on looking for new clients too.

So to sum up, clients aren't getting the experience they want from lawyers, and many don't even use a lawyer for their legal issues. At the same time, lawyers are working hard to find more clients and would spend more time on it if they could.

There's a huge gap here, but the solution is simple: If lawyers focused on giving clients the simplified experience they wanted, their clients would be happier, more likely to engage with a lawyer, and more likely to encourage others to do so as well. All of this would mean better reviews and more referrals for law firms, improving bottom lines. Law firms need to change their business models to match an environment where experience is king.

There's no shortage of research to show that developing an effortless client experience is one of the best investments a business can make:

- An overwhelming 86% of consumers would pay more for a better customer experience, according to Oracle's Customer Experience Impact Report.

- Adobe's 2018 Digital Trends report found that "organizations with 'a cohesive plan, long-term view, and executive support for the future of their customer' are more than twice as likely as their peers to significantly outperform their competitors (27% vs. 13%)."

- Nearly two-thirds (61%) of consumers agreed they feel loyal to brands that tailor experiences to their preferences and needs, per the Reinventing Loyalty report by Goldsmiths University and Adobe.

- According to RightNow's Customer Experience Impact Report, 55% of consumers would be willing to recommend a company based on their outstanding service—and this was more important than the company's product or its price. (An important factor since according to the 2019 Legal Trends Report, 59% of consumers seek a referral of some kind when they're looking to hire a lawyer.)

Provide a better experience by paying attention to what your legal clients *truly* need, and you'll generate more revenue, outperform your competitors, and earn more positive referrals. Ignore what your clients want, and your firm may go the way of Blockbuster. Apps, robots, and non-lawyer legal service providers won't replace law firms anytime soon—but law firms that leverage these tools to provide a better customer experience will become the norm, and law firms that stick to pen and paper and take two days to call a client back will find themselves struggling.

The world is changing. Your clients know a better experience is possible, and they expect it everywhere—even from their law firm. They use Google and instant messaging apps and online credit card payments every day, which means they notice when a law firm hasn't bothered to adopt those technologies. People used to be willing to play phone tag but now—with options like texting and online scheduling tools— clients are more discerning about such inconveniences.

There's an emotional aspect to this change in expectations as well. When you're forced to chase down your lawyer, or wait in the rain for a ride, or book a hotel room without knowing what you're going to get, it feels disappointing, and as a customer, you don't feel valued. The idea that someone couldn't be bothered to make your experience painless, or that they've actively engineered things to be more convenient for their organization at your expense, leads many consumers to choose an alternative service provider next time. Conversely, when someone provides an experience that *is* geared toward your needs, it isn't just more convenient. Someone gets you. Someone cared enough to make an everyday experience a bit easier for you. In many cases, you might not notice this type of experience when it's there, but this thoughtfulness builds a subtle but important trust that keeps you coming back—and you'll certainly notice when it's missing.

It's entirely possible for your law firm to capitalize on this need for a better client experience, and just like Netflix, Uber, and Airbnb discovered in their respective marketplaces, there's a massive competitive advantage waiting for the firm that embraces this thinking.

"

———

There's a huge gap here,

but the solution is simple:

If lawyers focused on giving

clients the simplified experience

they wanted, their clients would

be happier, more likely to

engage with a lawyer, and more

likely to encourage others

to do so as well.

———

"

2

UNLOCKING THE LATENT LEGAL MARKET

IN THIS ERA where the client experience reigns supreme, providing a cohesive, effortless legal experience across the whole client journey is essential for success. Firms that fail to embrace this new reality risk being left behind as people flock to client-centered competitors. Law firms that *do* focus on providing better legal experiences and giving clients what they want will discover the opportunity to unlock tremendous latent demand.

Law Is Not a Zero-Sum Game

In the examples we explored in Chapter 1—Netflix disrupted Blockbuster, Airbnb disrupted the hotel industry, and Uber disrupted the taxi industry—it's tempting to assume that there was a fixed amount of demand in each industry, and that the newcomer ate the incumbent's lunch. But that's not the case: These companies unlocked latent demand by connecting with the people who weren't constantly renting movies, staying in hotels, or taking taxis. They didn't steal a piece of the pie—they made the whole pie bigger.

When Blockbuster went bankrupt in 2010, Netflix's revenues were sitting around $2 billion, much lower than the roughly $6 billion in revenue that Blockbuster had while Netflix was still finding its footing. Today, Netflix has revenues of over $20 billion. It's created a market over three times larger than what Blockbuster ever enjoyed.

In New York City, the average number of daily trips by taxis has gone down as pickups using ridesharing apps has jumped. But overall, the average number of trips taken per day by taxi *and* rideshare combined grew from about 500,000 in 2010 to about 1 million per day in 2019. Ridesharing companies like Uber are reaching a larger market of people.

Airbnb's year-over-year growth in online bookings didn't cause a downturn in the year-over-year growth in bookings for hotels: Demand has continued to grow year-over-year for hotels *and* short-term vacation rentals, despite Airbnb adding significant supply to the market. (By 2017, Airbnb's 4 million listings outnumbered the rooms available from the world's top five hotel chains combined.) Airbnb has not killed hotels.

None of these three scenarios is a zero-sum game. It isn't a zero-sum game for law either. As much as there's a risk of losing business by ignoring the need to become a client-centered law firm, there's an opportunity to unlock latent demand and grow the legal market as a whole.

"

None of these three scenarios is a zero-sum game. It isn't a zero-sum game for law either.

"

A Short History of the Latent Legal Market

Richard Susskind talks about the coming emergence of a vast, latent legal market in his 1996 book *The Future of Law*. Over 20 years ago, he predicted that technology would transform the legal industry and the way legal services are delivered, and that more clients would enthusiastically adopt services that were cheaper, faster, or better able to meet their needs.

In 2001, a business writer for the *Denver Post* profiled successful self-legal-help companies, such as Nolo, that turned to the internet to access latent markets. Courts were on board with the creative delivery of legal services as well, with those in Denver and Colorado Springs providing self-help centers for pro se clients staffed by volunteer lawyers.

Interestingly, in 1998, the State Bar of Texas had tried to block such companies from operating, claiming that their books and software constituted the unauthorized practice of law. It argued that lawyers were the only ones who should be able to operate legal services, but Nolo argued that all Texans should have a right to basic legal information and that lawyers should not be able to ban competition. Eventually, the crusade against Nolo was quashed when the Texas Legislature exempted books and other self-help products from unauthorized practice of law rules, so long as they included a clear disclaimer that they did not constitute legal advice. In other words, lawyers have been losing their monopoly on the legal market for more than 30 years.

Commenting on the matter at the time, Thomas D. Russell, a legal historian and law professor at the University of Texas in Austin, said, "writing a will is not brain surgery … and living trusts simply are not as complicated as lawyers want them to be. Obviously that's a lucrative business, and the lawyers resent that people can do it on their own. I think that lawyers who oppose Nolo Press simply have to face the fact that *if software can do a lawyer's job, we don't need the lawyer.*" (Emphasis mine.)

As lawyers everywhere continued to staunchly advocate that they should provide sole access to the law, the disconnect between this belief and how the public viewed legal matters grew. In 2010, an article in the *Guardian* covered the findings of a survey by the Legal Services Research Centre and the University College of London: Only 44% of people would seek a lawyer to help with a legal issue, but only 11% would seek help for a problem that they didn't see as a legal issue, even if the issue *could* be handled legally (think noisy neighbors, faulty products or services, or children's education issues). For issues related to things such as debt and employment, some would attempt to go elsewhere for advice even if they *did* see their issue as a legal one.

Eight years later, when we conducted surveys for the *2018 Legal Trends Report*, this pattern continued: 57% of those surveyed said they had had an issue that could have been handled legally but wasn't, and only 22% said they'd prefer using the law to handle an issue whenever possible; 31% said using a lawyer was too costly, 35% said the benefits didn't justify the cost, and 28% didn't like not knowing the final cost of a service.

Over three-quarters of people in the US didn't seek a lawyer for help when they could have or should have, according to a 2018 report from the World Justice Project—even more so in other countries. These would-be legal clients are not using lawyers to solve their issues.

The Latent Legal Market Today

As of 2016, the size of the US legal market was about $437 billion annually, and market demand for legal services has stayed relatively flat: the *2019 Report on the State of the Legal Market* from Georgetown Law and Thomson Reuters Legal Executive Institute found that demand for legal services grew 1.3% in 2018, with this growth focused among larger law firms. But imagine how immense the legal market could be if lawyers connected with the people currently not seeking legal help because of poor product-market fit.

To use the iceberg analogy, the market worth upwards of $437 billion is what's visible from the surface, but there's so much more below the surface. There's the 77% of people in the US who didn't get legal help for their legal issues in 2018, according to the World Justice Project. There's the 57% of people who've dealt with a life issue that could have been handled legally but wasn't, according to the *Legal Trends Report*.

And there's the average American who would struggle to handle an unexpected $400 expense. A May 2019 report from the US Federal Reserve found that almost 40% of Americans couldn't cover an unexpected expense of $400: 27% would borrow money or sell something to cover the expense, and 12% wouldn't be able to cover the expense at all. The average billable hourly rate charged by law firms in the US is $253 per hour, according to the *2019 Legal Trends Report,* or more than half of that difficult-to-deal-with $400 expense. As it's doubtful that a legal issue could be resolved with an hour and a half of billable work, this pricing is completely out of step with the needs of the average American consumer.

There's a massive chasm between the pricing offered by lawyers and what the potential legal market is able to afford, and both parties lose out as a result. Law firms are missing out on a *ton* of potential clients, and would-be clients are missing out on access to legal services. Cost can always be a prohibitive factor for consumers, but this becomes problematic when it has created a barrier to services that are critical to society, including legal and even medical services. How would you feel if a family member facing a life-altering legal challenge didn't get help because they couldn't afford it?

If innovative legal practitioners can create a better product-market fit between the services lawyers offer and how consumers want (or need) to buy them—for example, by making services more efficient and affordable—they'll gain more clients and grow their firms like never before.

Pre-Emptive Adaptation

Services such as Nolo, Rocket Lawyer, and LegalZoom are not eating lawyers' lunches. There's no reason that innovation in the legal market can't come from law firms as well. To capture the latent demand for legal services and enjoy more clients and healthier revenues, law firms need to let go of the old model.

In other industries, old-guard companies have successfully made parallel adaptations. Take *The Atlantic*, for example, whose comeback story was chronicled in a 2011 Mashable article, among other places. In 1999, *The Atlantic* was a 142-year-old monthly magazine with a strong reputation, but it was struggling to survive in the dawning digital age, as readers turned more and more attention online. David

Bradley purchased the publication that year, and it continued to lose up to $8 million per year—until he hired Justin Smith as president of Atlantic Consumer Media in 2007.

Justin pushed the company to adopt a digital-first strategy, transforming it from a magazine with a website to a digital publisher that happened to continue publishing its long-running print magazine. In January 2008, the company removed its paywall from theatlantic.com, making its content freely available to website visitors and dramatically growing its online audience, from 500,000 unique visitors per month prior to the paywall drop to upwards of 11 million per month by 2011. (By June 2017, that number had risen to 42.3 million.)

In March 2008, the company's sales team was informed that their digital and print ad targets would no longer be separate. By 2010, *The Atlantic* was profitable again, bringing in $1.8 million. Digital went from earning 9% of ad revenue to making a projected 45% of revenues in 2011, but notably, this didn't kill its print advertising revenues—most ad buyers wanted both digital *and* print representation, and as a result, print ad revenues grew by 24% in 2010. Justin Smith attributed this dual success to an increase in brand presence driven by *The Atlantic*'s online success: As theatlantic.com began to receive millions of monthly visitors, more and more people became aware of the print magazine. The company has continued to adapt and innovate, and at over 160 years old, founded by the likes of Ralph Waldo Emerson and Harriet Beecher Stowe, it's still going strong as one of the top 50 news sites on the web—oh, and the magazine is still in print with a total circulation of 474,274 subscriptions as of June 2019.

Leaders at *The Atlantic* saw their industry changing and wholeheartedly dove into an innovative approach. Rather than simply trying to prolong the slow but inevitable decline into irrelevance for a print-only publication, they shifted their focus to where the majority of their customers (readers) had migrated—online—and *both* the old product and the new one thrive as a result.

Jordan Furlong mentioned *The Atlantic* story in a 2009 blog post entitled "How to Kill a Law Firm," and in it, he cited the following quote from Justin Smith: "'If our mission was to kill the magazine, what would we do?' said Smith, who added that a digital competitor was going to do that anyway, so they did it themselves." Jordan's point is that law firms should be asking themselves the same question and then taking that action: Do what those trying to "kill" law firms would do— before your competitors.

For law firms willing to pay attention to the potential clients they're missing and adapt to give them what they need, there's an opportunity not just to survive but to thrive and to help define what it means to practice law and run a law firm in today's world.

Accessing the Latent Legal Market

Price alone is a very concrete barrier for thousands of would-be legal clients—and that's just *one* facet of the broader client experience that, when delivered in a way that doesn't match client demand, leads potential clients to not use law firms at all. There are other levers that we'll explore in later chapters that law firms can (and must) pull to better match existing demand for legal services, get more clients, and thrive in this age of experience. It's about giving your would-be clients what they *really* want.

Take Aldi, for example, a German grocery chain known for its low prices. Aldi focuses ruthlessly on what its customers care about and cuts out what they don't. The stores set out products in their original cardboard shipping boxes, eschewing attractive displays in favor of saved time. Customers pay a 25-cent deposit for shopping carts, pay for their own bags, and bag their own groceries, and they don't mind, because the groceries cost less.

The footprint for most Aldi stores is also smaller than an average grocery store, stocking far fewer items (1,400 items, compared to a typical 40,000), and you won't find many familiar name brands on the shelves. But customers actually like this—less selection means less hemming and hawing over which brand of cereal to buy, so customers get in and out of the store faster. The aisles at Aldi are extra wide so carts can pass each other easily. 90% of the products that Aldi sells are Aldi's own brand, and the store designs its packaging with extra barcodes for faster scanning to keep lines moving. Everything at Aldi is designed to give its customers what they want: to save money on their groceries and to do groceries as quickly as possible. Notice that what customers want isn't a delightful trip to the grocery store.

Focusing intently on what its customers want—and not on what they don't care about—has led Aldi to succeed as its competitors have struggled or filed for bankruptcy. Technically made up of two chains operating in 18 countries, Aldi brought in combined sales of $98 billion for 2017, making it the world's eighth largest retailer by revenue, according to Deloitte. It's

> *Who would use your services if they were a little less pricey, if the price was predictable up-front, or if clients felt more informed about their legal issue before they hired you? That's the latent legal market your firm isn't addressing yet.*

also set to be the third largest chain of grocery stores in the US, with 2,500 stores planned to be opened by 2022.

No matter how big or small your law firm is, no matter what type of law you practice, this type of client-centered focus can bring success for your law firm as well. Think about who your potential clients *really* are and what they *really* want. Who would use your services if they were a little less pricey, if the price was predictable up-front, or if clients felt more informed about their legal issue before they hired you? That's the latent legal market your firm isn't addressing yet.

Some firms are already addressing this market in creative ways. DLA Piper, frequently recognized as one of the most innovative law firms in multiple jurisdictions, has launched a myriad of initiatives to better meet client needs and address latent markets. For example, the firm's Accelerate website offers information for early stage companies and tools for companies to generate various legal documents for free. DLA Piper thus builds relationships with potential clients that otherwise might have perceived DLA Piper as out-of-reach. The firm has also created its own proprietary tool, Ascendant 2.0, to help clients streamline the bidding process and complete transactional projects faster.

Client-centered innovation isn't just for Am Law 100 firms with big tech budgets. Palace Law, a Tacoma-based personal injury firm, came up with an innovative approach to help would-be clients who otherwise wouldn't see a lawyer. With the help of LawDroid, the firm created what it calls PatBot, a chatbot that helps assess worker compensation claims. The bot informs users that it's not a lawyer and doesn't offer legal advice, but it assesses their claims with a detailed Q&A, highlights any issues and the law surrounding them, and provides tools such as forms, letters, and further information so that the injured person can make an informed decision about whether to handle the issue themselves or get help from a lawyer. The creators call this output a "Legal Health Check," and it's provided for free—but the bot is also embedded in Palace Law's website, with the firm's branding and a contact phone number clearly displayed in the upper-right corner of the screen. Clients who use PatBot and *do* decide they need a lawyer certainly know where to turn next.

Both DLA Piper and Palace Law are creatively addressing the needs of clients who otherwise might not use their services. If your law firm is just starting out with such innovation, addressing the latent market doesn't have to be complicated. Use online forms to streamline your client intake. Use a cloud-based portal to allow clients to access their own case information, empowering them and reducing follow-up for you. Send invoices online to ensure clients get their bills when they expect them, and cut out the time and money spent on postage and stuffing envelopes.

I often get asked, "If you make law firms more efficient with lower prices, won't that shrink the market?" That's only true if you look at the legal market as a finite and fixed number of billable hours and clients. By not only lowering prices, but also packaging legal services in a more client-centered way, law firms can unlock a total addressable market that is much larger than the market that exists today. With a client-centered mindset, enabled by the right tech, innovative law firms will connect with the multitudes of people currently unserved. The time to adopt such a client-centered mindset is now.

3

THE TIME IS NOW

CONSUMERS DON'T THINK lawyers are special. In the eyes of your clients, there's no category set aside for lawyers that exempts them from providing a good client experience. Still, there's a persistent story that lawyers *are* different, that they're outside the new reality of an experience-driven world as a result of their subject-matter expertise, intelligence, and dedication needed to practice law. It might sting to hear it, but this simply isn't true.

Now more than ever, clients *do* have other options when it comes to getting their legal issues dealt with—and those options are growing. For law firms who want to survive and thrive in a client-centered world, it's now time to adapt.

Lawyers Aren't Different

Consider that doctors, like lawyers, are highly educated, highly esteemed professionals. Yet when people are looking for a new family doctor, they don't choose someone based on how they ranked in their class at medical school. They want to know that their new doctor will be competent enough to help them, and beyond that, they'll choose someone based on the level of experience they provide. Recognition of this has led to plenty of innovations in the way the medical industry works. You can now see a doctor via video, have birth control delivered to your door, or have doctors come to your home.

It's the same with lawyers. The baseline expectation is that you'll be able to complete your work competently, and any differentiation between the concrete legal deliverable you'd provide and the deliverable from another lawyer three blocks down the street is, in many cases, virtually nonexistent.

Graduating at the top of your class and working to be the best-of-the-best when compared to other lawyers in terms of your legal acumen is *one* way to stand out to clients. But realistically, for most lawyers, that's an incredibly competitive path with a high chance of failure. The law school you graduated from, or your legal ability alone, won't be enough for a client to choose you over someone else. Investing in a client-centered approach, and providing better client experiences, gives you a *much* better value for your time and effort, and your probability of standing out is a lot higher.

The Risk of Being Too Risk Averse

Lawyers are notoriously risk averse, and in many contexts, they're right to be that way. Their job is to think carefully and critically about every situation they come across and ensure all angles are covered. Lawyers must also stay compliant with strict industry regulations and ethics rules. One misstep can lead to a malpractice suit or even disbarment. But sometimes, being risk averse is the real risk.

Take the use of technology in law firms, for example. Many law firms are still exclusively using pen and paper. But there are ethics rules that require lawyers to educate themselves and stay open to change. For example, Comment 8 to Rule 1.1 of the ABA's Model Rules of Professional Conduct used to state that "a lawyer should keep abreast of changes in the law and its practice," but in 2012, the comment was amended to add "including the benefits and risks associated with relevant technology." So far, 38 US states have adopted the revised comment. Importantly, this amendment wasn't introduced to add a requirement that lawyers stay informed on the benefits and risks of technology. It was introduced to *clarify* that lawyers had always had that responsibility.

Clio was founded with the goal of using technology to help lawyers mitigate risk. My cofounder Rian and I learned from a friend that solo lawyers and small law firms in British Columbia were struggling to keep their firms organized. Data-entry errors and missed deadlines were leading to ethics complaints, and some lawyers were even being disbarred. Large law firms had key infrastructure, including software, paralegals, and support staff, to help them keep track of these things—but the cost for on-premise solutions alone was tens of thousands of dollars, not to mention the additional costs of IT support and internal servers. Many small firms couldn't afford these solutions.

A secure, cloud-based program is an affordable way to help lawyers keep themselves on-track. When we launched Clio at the 2008 ABA TECHSHOW, many were skeptical of the cloud, but many more were excited to have such a solution available. In fact, our very first customer, Catherine Merino Reisman, thought it was clearly beneficial to switch to the cloud. She didn't want to have to hire an IT person, get a server set up, and safeguard it from the world, and she reasoned that she wouldn't have the money and resources to keep firm data as secure as a company like Clio could.

Today, the use of the cloud is table stakes across many industries, due to the better scalability, collaboration, and security available. But the legal industry has still been relatively slow to adopt it. The ABA's 2018 *TECHREPORT* found that 54.6% of firms were using the cloud in their practices—low compared to the 94% of organizations using the cloud in the broader business world. For those unfamiliar, "the cloud" covers any type of service you'd access through the internet—everything from social media and email, to practice management and customer relationship management (CRM) software. You're likely using the cloud in your personal life, even if you're not using it in your practice yet.

Not every new technology, business model, or management technique is right for every law practice, but bias against *any* sort of change is the real risk. Technology adoption is just one example of how the legal industry can take too conservative a stance and fall behind.

The mindset that accepts as status quo practices such as taking two days to call clients back, charging fees with little regard to what makes sense for clients, and keeping paper copies of everything is holding law firms back. The legal industry is at an inflection point, and lawyers who haven't adopted a more client-centered mindset yet need to do so now.

Increasing Competition

Clients have more and more options when it comes to getting their legal needs met. Publishers like Nolo have been around for decades, but other legal alternatives have entered the industry more recently—and they're growing aggressively. Clients, it seems, are all too happy to work with non-law firms to get their legal needs met, especially when the experience is better.

The well-documented rise of alternative legal service providers (ALSPs) speaks to this increasing demand for more client-centered legal services: Overall, revenues for ALSPs grew from $8.4 billion in 2015 to $10.7 billion in 2017. ALSPs are companies that provide certain legal services—such as legal research, contract management, and document review—in more systematic, efficient ways than a traditional law firm would. ALSPs have gained favor with corporate clients because their legal needs are met while costs are kept down.

Far from being a fringe or nascent idea, ALSPs have established a booming industry. Axiom, which focuses on providing the talent and technology that legal departments need to succeed, reported revenues of $300 million in 2017. With 2,000 employees across three continents, it spun off two of its businesses in early 2019 and earned a "significant" investment from European private equity firm Permira later that year. Its clients include Dell, PayPal, and Coca-Cola.

In September 2018, UnitedLex, which bills itself as an enterprise legal services provider, sold a majority stake in its business to CVC Capital Partners for $500 million. As of that date, the company counted 25% of the Global Fortune 500 as its clients and reported closing deals worth $1.5 billion in the 18 months prior.

Elevate Services, which calls itself "the law company," projected it would reach up to $90 million in gross revenue for 2019 early that year and has acquired a number of other consulting and managed services businesses.

Then there are the Big Four: Deloitte, Ernst & Young, PricewaterhouseCoopers, and KPMG. In recent years, these firms have started to encroach on the legal industry by offering legal services. And they make a compelling offer: Mark Cohen of Legal Mosaic puts it well, explaining that while many may still view the Big Four as accounting firms, they call themselves "professional services networks" and constantly expand their offerings to match the needs of their clients. With long-trusted brand names, deep pockets, and existing relationships with corporate leaders, they're positioned to succeed. Sure, the Big Four still have some catching up to do in terms of revenue compared to the world's largest law firms (PwC earned $500 million from legal services in 2016, while leading firm Latham & Watkins earned $2.8 billion), but according to a 2019 report from Thomson Reuters and Georgetown Law, 20% of large law firms reported competing against the Big Four the year prior, suggesting these (not solely) accounting heavyweights are on a growth track that just won't quit.

This is a taste of what's going on in the legal market. There are many different types of ALSPs out there, and other trends such as increased insourcing by corporate legal departments indicate that corporate clients are taking advantage of alternatives over law firms.

And it isn't only business clients who are looking further afield for legal services. Alternative legal options are on the rise for consumers as well. While some still oppose the idea that companies such as LegalZoom—which allows users to create legal documents without a lawyer—should be allowed to exist, LegalZoom is alive and well and growing. It settled with the North Carolina State Bar in 2015, meaning that it's allowed to continue operating in that state, and the company received a $500 million investment in July 2018. At the time, it was valued at roughly $2 billion. John Suh, former CEO and now senior advisor at LegalZoom, recognizes that for most people, accessing legal services is a chore rather than something to get excited about, so he focused on making the experience of using legal services as painless as possible. Instead of hiring a lawyer for an hourly rate, users of LegalZoom choose the level of help they need for a set price. For example, if clients are creating a will, they can self-serve by answering questions and following the instructions on the site. Or they can sign up for an estate plan bundle that includes a year of attorney advice to discuss and review their estate plan. For packages that involve more specific legal services, such as those included in LegalZoom's attorney-led trademark application package, the company clearly explains why a lawyer is recommended and what they'll be doing, so clients know the value they're getting and what to expect *before* they get legal help.

Contrast that with the experience of hiring a lawyer but being given little idea about what the process will be like and no guarantee of what the final cost will be, and it's clear why this option works so much better for consumers. The success of ALSPs confirms that legal clients want simpler, more painless experiences and that they'll enthusiastically embrace a departure from tradition to get them.

Time to Act

Despite the realities of consumer demand in the legal space, law firms have been relatively slow to change.

There has been plenty of discussion about whether billing by the hour makes sense for modern clients, but the billable hour remains a stubborn fixture for law firms—even though this model isn't efficient for lawyers themselves. The *2019 Legal Trends Report* found that the average lawyer worked just 2.5 hours of billable work each day in 2018, with 19% of that time not making it to the final bill, and 15% of hours invoiced never getting paid. Meanwhile, for 28% of consumers, not knowing the final cost of their legal engagement is a barrier to hiring a lawyer at all. Firms also remain notoriously slow to implement new tech. A 2018 study from Gartner found that 81% of corporate legal departments are unprepared to support digital initiatives within their organizations. Meanwhile, most law firms still aren't using practice management software to manage their firms: According to the ABA's 2018 *TECHREPORT*, adoption of practice management systems is holding steady at around 30% for firms of all sizes. The same report found only 10% of lawyers are currently using AI for legal work.

Law firms that stand still risk falling behind as alternative providers and innovative law firms leverage new technologies to provide legal solutions aligned more closely with what clients need. The time to act is now—look at this as an opportunity. The fact that many law firms have yet to implement tech and adopt client-centered thinking means that these are still powerful levers forward-thinking law firms can pull to become more competitive. Firms have a chance to adapt to the needs of modern clients and access a huge amount of latent demand in the legal market. You don't have to be a canary in a coal mine.

There's space for evolution in the industry, and technology provides a useful lens for explaining why I believe that, despite years of change in the legal industry, the need for law firms to provide better client experiences has never been as urgent as it is now.

> *The time to act is now—*
> *look at this as an opportunity:*
> *The fact that many law firms have*
> *yet to implement tech and adopt*
> *client-centered thinking means*
> *that these are still powerful levers*
> *forward-thinking law firms can*
> *pull to become more competitive.*

Running a client-centered law firm isn't about using technology (yes, I say that as a tech CEO). Client-centered thinking—which I'll explain in detail in the next chapter—is a mental model to help you make decisions that benefit both your clients and your firm, by providing an experience that aligns with what your client actually wants, not a siren call to throw tech at the problem.

That said, as long as firms put their clients at the center of their thinking, tech often *does* end up being at least part of solutions that lead to good experiences. The key is for lawyers to think about using tech to meet client needs in creative ways, not merely to work faster. Richard Susskind put it well in *Tomorrow's Lawyers*. He states, "There is a profound message here for lawyers—when thinking about IT and the internet, the challenge is not just to automate current working practices that are not efficient. The challenge is to innovate, to practice law in ways that we could not have done in the past." Think online forms that mean clients don't have to leave the house to visit their divorce lawyer when they're feeling extremely upset about their separation, or ediscovery driven by predictive coding that keeps costs down for your GC and helps her look good in front of the CEO. Technology empowers law firms to solve client problems more effectively by *supporting* client-centered processes.

When adopting a new technology, there are a lot of unknowns, and there's often an instinct to hesitate. Sometimes, that instinct is well placed. Other times, it can mean the difference between gaining compounding advantages for your business and being left behind.

In its early days, promoting your business on Facebook was fairly affordable. You could build a community that liked your page and have them see your posts for free, and ads on the platform were relatively cheap. But as the network's user base grew, more and more businesses flocked to Facebook advertising, and users complained about seeing too many ads in their feeds. As a result, Facebook now constantly tweaks its algorithm to determine which posts and ads show up in someone's feed, and increasing demand for ad space has meant that ad costs are constantly on the rise. Today, any business worth its salt is still advertising on Facebook. High costs, restrictive algorithms, and Cambridge Analytica scandals aside, Facebook is still the world's largest social media network. But it's much more expensive to build a brand presence on Facebook today than it was early on, and those that invested early enjoy a sustained advantage. They were able to corner the market, at least for a short while. To be clear, I'm not suggesting you go out and find the next great social media platform and go all in on advertising your law firm there. But I am suggesting that you look closely before you label a new mindset, tool, or business model as risky.

Alternative options for meeting legal needs simply aren't as risky as they once were. Connie Brenton, former chair of the Corporate Legal Operations Consortium (CLOC) said, "When a Fortune 500 GC sees that 46% of their peers have leveraged [a legal service outsource firm], it is not risky any longer." She said that back in 2017, when the most recent CLOC State of the Industry survey had found that nearly half of all Fortune 500 companies had used at least one alternative legal services provider.

This isn't a trend we're only seeing in the world of ALSPs and large firms servicing corporate legal clients either: A 30% adoption rate for practice management systems for firms of all sizes is not a majority by any means, but it's also far from zero. Not everyone has adopted tech yet—but law firms are starting to. And for good reason. On-premise systems that helped firms stay organized used to cost tens of thousands of dollars, but today, any law firm can access a smorgasbord of legal tools that cost on the order of $100 per month. Adopting a client-centered mindset, and providing better experiences with the help of technology, is more accessible than it's ever been.

Change in the legal industry isn't *going* to happen. It's happening *now*, and it has been happening for some time. There's still an opportunity to adopt a model that's more resilient in the face of modern corporate and consumer expectations, but the window will close faster than you think. We're at a sweet spot where there's a lower risk and a maximum reward. The legal industry as a whole has been slow to change, which means your practice, and your career, could still realize outsized benefits from the early-ish adoption of a client-centered model.

A useful way to think about this is in terms of the Gartner Hype Cycle, a visualization created by research and advisory company Gartner to help investors think through the benefits and risks of new technologies over time. The idea is that the impacts of a technology are likely to be overhyped and overestimated early on, and underrecognized and underestimated later. Gartner highlights five stages along the cycle: the Innovation Trigger, the Peak of Inflated Expectations, the Trough of Disillusionment, the Slope of Enlightenment, and the Plateau of Productivity.

Law firms are still early in the hype cycle for adoption of legal technologies and client-centered models—but not *that* early. The Big Four, other ALSPs, and innovative law firms have proven that more client-centered models are successful.

We're early, but we're also definitely past the point of risk and into a place of confirmed commercial viability within the cycle—at the very start of the slope of enlightenment.

The way many law firms operate today, and what constitutes a competitive firm in the eyes of the majority, will look very different 10 years from now. Law firms looking to differentiate themselves have a significant window in which they can execute on client-centered strategies and gain the advantage of getting comfortable with this change now, but as time goes on, they'll more likely have to play catch up.

For law firms that haven't already started operating with their clients at the center of their thinking, this is a critical moment: Will you be part of a sea change in the legal industry, or will you, your practice, and your livelihood miss out?

Becoming a Legal Changemaker

Earlier in this chapter, I talked about how lawyers are often risk averse. If they do things the way they always have, then there's no risk of getting slapped with a malpractice suit because they tried something new. But the truth is everything covered in this chapter and in this book is fair game. We're not talking about bleeding-edge technologies with questionable ethical implications. We're talking about established ALSPs and tools already used by plenty of clients *and* law firms.

One big lesson I've learned over the past 10-plus years working with lawyers is that they don't want to be first, especially when it comes to new or different business models. They'd much rather see someone else test the waters before they dip their toes in themselves. But they also don't want to be last. Most lawyers have a competitive streak that makes the idea of being the absolute last off the mark anathema to them.

Good news: The opportunity to be the first law firm to try an innovative, client-centered approach has passed. These days, it's easy to find examples of firms succeeding with a client-centered approach—as you'll continue to see throughout this book—but there's still a tremendous opportunity to be a part of the movement that transforms the legal industry.

The change necessary to help law firms become more client-centered, connect with more clients, and succeed in an experience-driven world won't be easy. It's going to take a full crew to change direction, but it is possible. A massive ship changes course slowly, and the mechanisms that kick off this change are so small as to be almost imperceptible in the grand scheme of things—but at a certain point, the ship is suddenly headed for a completely different continent.

It all starts with legal professionals like you becoming legal changemakers. Partners, associates, paralegals, legal assistants, receptionists, and law students will have a powerful role to play in sparking the client-centered revolution. Whether you're a solo practitioner or you're at a firm of 1,000 or more people, you can spark the change that helps law firms thrive in an experience-driven world.

Maybe you want to better serve your local community by providing more affordable services. Maybe you often see your clients stressed out and upset and you've identified a few small ways to make their experience a little more painless. Maybe you're in a position to advocate for more innovation at a larger firm—and see results that resonate with your clients and fellow outside counsels. Whatever your role, you have a chance—now—to be a part of the client-centered revolution.

Running a client-centered law firm isn't just about providing better client experiences, getting positive reviews, and garnering more referrals either. It's about creating a more pleasant work environment for yourself and your staff. The old adage of "happy employees make happy customers" is true, but it goes further than that: A study of 5,000 individuals over nearly 20 years found that "people's happiness depends on the happiness of others with whom they are connected." In other words, happiness most definitely is contagious.

While it's not talked about as openly as it should be, there's a serious emotional cost that comes with being a lawyer. As lawyer and legal mindfulness expert Jeena Cho puts it, "Lawyers are in the trauma business. Rarely do clients come to see us with happy news." Lawyers face an onslaught of other stressors too. From the time you enter law school, there's pressure to be perfect—to get straight A's, just like you did all through your undergraduate degree, through high school, and maybe even further back than that. There's pressure to be a part of extracurricular activities and to get a good placement during the summer, because that will lead to good entry-level positions later on and that could define your entire career—or ruin it, if you don't get the position you want. And once you're practicing? Well, your clients are trusting you with some of the most important challenges of their lives! You can't get it wrong—you're a lawyer! Plus if you want to make partner, you've got to prove, once again, that you're the best of the best.

Lawyers face a massive amount of pressure to be superhuman, or at least to appear that way on the outside—to always be the expert and to never remove their armor. But when lawyers are willing to be a bit vulnerable and open to the idea that changing the way they run their businesses might lead to better balance and more of what they love, amazing things can happen. In short, clients aren't the only ones who need change in the legal industry—lawyers need it too. Given that the legal profession faces high rates of depression, stress, and anxiety, an approach to running a law firm that improves the environment for staff, lawyers, *and* clients is worth investing in.

Lawyers who think intently about the client experience are not lowering their standards, or prioritizing being a business-person over perfecting their craft. They're making changes so that the client experience side of their firm runs more smoothly, and they can focus even more on the practice of law. Those who join in shifting to a client-centered approach will have a say in what law firms of the experience-driven future look like, and what it will mean to practice law.

Change is already happening, but we can't lose momentum. We need legal changemakers who are passionate about transforming the practice of law, for good, to stand up and advocate for innovative ideas, no matter what their position is within their firm. We need you to stand up for what's best for clients and create a healthy working environment. It's my firm belief that lawyers and their clients deserve this and much more.

4

DON'T PUT YOUR CLIENTS FIRST

BY THIS POINT, I hope I've convinced you of the necessity for change in the legal industry, that today's consumers demand an experience that puts them at the center, and that law firms that fail to adapt to this reality risk being left out in the cold. However, adapting to this reality doesn't mean putting your clients first. In fact, my opinion is that you absolutely *shouldn't* put your clients first.

Client-First or Client-Centered?

En route to the 2019 ABA TECHSHOW, one of our customers tweeted that she'd accidentally flushed her Apple AirPods down the airplane toilet. One of our staff noticed the tweet and, not wanting one of our customers to have a less-than-stellar conference experience, suggested we surprise her with a new pair of AirPods. After a bit of coordination and a lot of searching, we caught up with her and were able to give her a new set of 'Pods. She was happy and excited. She shared her story with others, and Clio was able to live up to its reputation of unabashedly giving a damn about its customers. But here's the thing: This customer doesn't continue to use Clio because we replaced her AirPods after an unfortunate mishap. She uses Clio because she needs to keep her practice organized, and she sees Clio as the best solution for that need.

In recent years, the idea to "surprise and delight" customers has become popular. When the stars align, you can certainly take advantage of opportunities to go above and beyond for your clients, and this definitely strengthens relationships. But too much of it can be expensive—imagine if we gave out free AirPods to any customer who was having a difficult day. That would add up quickly! And, more critically, it would divert our focus from delivering the core experience our customers expect from us.

When you put one thing first, by definition, other things have to come second, third, and so on. It's a linear model of prioritization. Your client comes first, and your firm, your staff, and you, come afterward, with the hope that bending over backward to give your client everything they could possibly want will provide long-term rewards.

You could think of client-first lawyering as a mental model intended to help you run a better business—but then you'd really be putting your business first, not your clients, wouldn't you? Client-first thinking is more nuanced than this, of course, but the main point is that there's a subtle yet powerful anchoring that happens when you think "client first," and it isn't necessarily helpful.

It's much more effective to treat clients as the hub for your decision-making. This helps your clients have an excellent experience, while also ensuring that the process changes you make are cost effective and logical. In a client-centered model, your client is at the core of what you do. All other aspects of your firm surround them, and any decisions being made cycle between the inner and outer layer.

Changes could be triggered by wanting something to work better at your law firm *first*—that just means the process should involve cycling back to the center and asking, "How will this decision affect my client's experience? Am I giving them what they truly need?" The reverse is true as well. If a change is triggered by wanting to make things better for your client *first*, the process needs to cycle outward: "How will this affect my staff and our processes? Is this efficient?"

THE CLIENT-CENTERED LAW FIRM

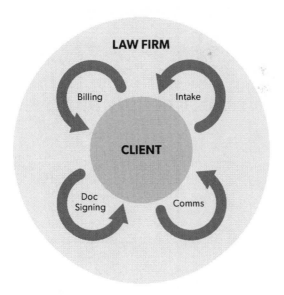

"

—————

Putting your clients
at the center of your thinking,
and running a client-centered
law firm, empowers you and
your firm to be profitable and
successful in a world where the
client experience is paramount.

—————

"

Clients are a key *part* of a client-centered law firm, and both pieces are necessary to make up the whole. Without a law firm around the exterior, clients don't have the protective layer of legal representation that they need—but without clients at the core, law firms are hollow and can't survive.

Putting your clients at the center of your thinking, and running a client-centered law firm, empowers you and your firm to be profitable and successful in a world where the client experience is paramount.

The Client-Centered Law Firm

With a client-centered mindset, you continually find opportunities to improve the way you operate for both you and your clients. Whether you're trying to overhaul a process that's broken or refine a process that's slightly inconvenient, thinking about how solutions affect both your firm and your clients will help you get to the best result.

Palace Law, the personal injury law firm in Tacoma, Washington, that created PatBot, was dealing with a high volume of phone calls from clients. Roughly 400 clients called about twice every two weeks. Needless to say, this level of call volume took a lot of time for staff to deal with, and the firm wanted to address client needs more efficiently. At first, they focused their attention on making it easy for clients to text them, thinking that a lower-effort option would reduce calls in favor of texting. However, this change didn't have much of an impact—Palace Law was still getting plenty of clients phoning in.

So Palace Law turned to their clients to ask *why* they were calling so often. It turned out that clients were calling up to three times a week for an update on whether a check had come in for them. Calling guaranteed them an immediate reply, so they didn't text. In response, Palace Law set up a system that automatically sends clients a text message as soon as their check is ready. No calling in or follow-up required.

Since implementing that solution, Palace Law takes only one to two of these types of calls per day—far lower than the hundreds of calls it used to receive per week. Staff at Palace Law now spend less time on the phone and more time on other tasks, thanks to this more efficient method. By asking questions and homing in on what clients truly wanted, while also thinking about what works best for the firm, Palace Law was able to create a better experience while also making its processes more efficient.

A client-*centered* law firm, rather than one where your clients come first or second, requires continually thinking about how the needs of the client and the firm overlap, and how these needs can be met in a way that creates the best possible experience for everyone. Palace Law takes this approach to every change it implements and has seen plenty of positive results. For example, a few changes to the firm's client intake system, including a switch from paper forms to a more paperless, automated system, resulted in a 76% increase in year-over-year revenue in just three quarters.

Running a client-centered firm *and* growing a profitable practice are not opposing goals. In fact, they drive each other.

Turning the Flywheel

If you put your clients at the center, focusing on them each time your firm makes a decision about how it operates, you'll create a flywheel effect that helps your firm grow and improve while also serving your clients better.

A flywheel is a mechanical device designed to resist changes in speed and smooth output from an erratic source of power, store energy, or deliver large bursts of energy. It takes a lot of energy to start a flywheel moving, but once you get it moving it seems virtually unstoppable.

The flywheel effect is a widely known concept in business, and one that we use to think about growth at Clio with incredible results. First conceptualized by Jim Collins in his book *Good to Great*, the effect refers to how an organization continues to make small decisions geared toward success, day in and day out, until one day, those efforts culminate in an unstoppable force that takes a good or mediocre business to greatness. Jim interviewed multiple public companies that he felt had made the leap from good to great to ask how they had gotten there and received very similar answers: They couldn't attribute their success to any one change or moment in time. Rather, it was a buildup of small changes that eventually paid off.

There is no one decision, no silver bullet that takes businesses—including law firms—from good to great. But, by relentlessly committing to a vision and acting on it, you "store up" that effort so that the eventual output is many times larger than you ever thought possible, allowing you to overcome seemingly insurmountable barriers. And if you keep pushing, your efforts keep compounding, and the wheel continues to spin faster.

A great example of the flywheel in action comes from Amazon. Of the businesses we draw lessons from for the legal industry, Amazon is one of the most powerful sources of inspiration. Jeff Bezos wrote the main tenets of Amazon's flywheel on the back of a napkin around 2011, and it looked something like this:

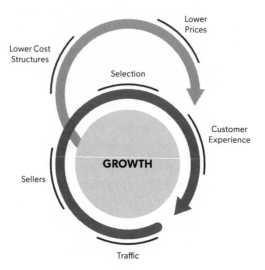

Amazon has always been customer-obsessed, but there's more to it than that: Providing a great customer experience helps turn Amazon's flywheel, which has driven the company's meteoric growth. Here's how it works: Focusing on lower prices and greater selection improves the customer experience, which drives more traffic to Amazon's site, which makes it more attractive to sellers, thereby allowing the company to sign on more retailers. In turn, this further improves selection, which improves the customer experience and accelerates the cycle of growth. As the company grows, its cost structures improve, which allows it to lower prices further, leading to an even better customer experience, which accelerates the cycle of growth even more. This has been described as a virtuous cycle of growth: Improve any point in the cycle, and the customer experience improves, which means the company grows faster. Today, at over $230 billion in annual revenue and with a 33% share of the US ecommerce market, Amazon is unstoppable. This is the flywheel effect in action.

Your law firm is not a public company hoping for massive growth and an uptick in its stock price, but if you're anything like the lawyers surveyed in the *Legal Trends Report*, you want more clients, so you do want *some* growth at your firm—or, at the very least, sustainability. Take a client-centered approach, and your firm can start pushing the flywheel to achieve growth.

Every time you make a change to improve the client experience, you push the flywheel for your law firm's success. Your next client is slightly happier with their experience. Those happier clients are more likely to leave you positive reviews online and tell their friends about you, which means more word-of-mouth referrals, which means more clients for your firm—and an overall improvement for your bottom line. In turn, this additional revenue enables you to invest in further improving the client experience.

The better the experience you provide, the stronger your reputation becomes, and the faster your law firm's flywheel turns. Whether you want to continuously grow your firm and get more clients, want the freedom to be selective about the cases your firm takes on, or want to raise your prices, pushing the flywheel will help your firm achieve that goal.

At the same time, this growth affords your firm better resources to invest in further refining processes to make them more efficient, improving your net profits as you improve the client experience.

THE LAW FIRM FLYWHEEL

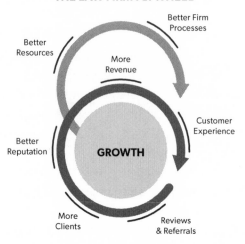

It's all driven by the client experience. Anything you can do to improve the client experience (while also improving your firm's internal processes) is worth an investment, because it adds up to a good reputation, more referrals, and more revenues.

Beginning might be hard. You might run up against resistance, and the new processes your firm employs might be confusing. The wheel is heavy and hard to turn at first, so it's critical to stay committed. But, as long as you're using a client-centered mindset, every time you improve something for your clients, you can improve something for staff and associates too, and vice versa—meaning that you're decreasing your operating costs and making the day-to-day of staff and lawyers more pleasant, while also improving your client growth and retention.

If clients prefer automatic updates to calling your firm once a week, chances are that staff don't enjoy providing updates over the phone either. And time-consuming phone calls take your staff away from other activities. Automatic updates are really better for everyone. It doesn't matter whether your clients or your staff drive your decision to make the change: With a client-centered mindset, you improve the lives of both, you uncover more opportunities, and the cycle continues. Better client intake means less stress for clients and less friction for your law firm. Better billing means clients have fewer questions and complaints, and staff spend less time on follow-up. Staff are happier and more productive because they're dealing with fewer tedious tasks at work, while clients have better experiences and are more likely to refer new business to your firm. Everyone feels a little bit more human because they're operating in an environment where their experience is seen as important and worth improving on—and your firm is more profitable, to boot. The flywheel turns faster.

How to Not Put Your Clients First

To run a law firm that's truly client-centered, it's critical to keep a mindset that is, in fact, client-*centered*, not client-first or firm-first. To avoid falling into one of these traps, you need to do two things:

1. Know what clients want.
2. Give clients what they want.

People are complex creatures. Figuring out what anyone wants and whether you're providing that to them takes a lot of research, thought, and attention. If knowing exactly what consumers want was easy, there'd be many more Amazons,

Netflixs, and Ubers in existence. With law firms, people are paying a higher price for a service they acutely need, rather than want, so the stakes for getting it right are high.

But going overboard for your clients isn't the answer—accuracy is. You can't give your clients what they want if it's not sustainable or efficient for your law firm, so it's important to focus on *meeting* expectations for your clients. The hard part is getting crystal clear on what those expectations are—and as we learned from Chapter 1, most law firms are currently getting it wrong.

Figuring Out What Your Clients Want

How do you like your coffee? Most people say they want a nice dark roast. In fact, according to famed psychophysicist Howard Moskowitz (you may recognize the name from Malcolm Gladwell's 2004 TED Talk), only 25–27% of people actually like their coffee this way—most people like weak, milky coffee.

People can't always clearly articulate what they want or need, and this goes for your legal clients too. A fundamental part of running a client-centered law firm is being attuned to your client's needs and expectations, but often this requires digging deeper than simply asking what they want. It means looking and listening for clues to find out what issue they're *really* trying to solve.

A good framework for thinking about this is the Jobs to be Done theory of innovation, first popularized by Harvard Business School professor Clayton Christensen. The idea is that people buy a given product or service not because they desperately *want* that product or service, but because they have a job they need to get done, and they're looking for the best solution available, whether that means convenience, quality, taste, effectiveness, or any other number of factors. Consider this popular quote from another Harvard Business School professor, Theodore Levitt, often referenced when describing Jobs to be Done theory (and by Richard Susskind at the start of many of his presentations): "People don't want to buy a quarter-inch drill, they want to buy a quarter-inch hole."

If you work at a law firm, clients are coming to you with their own versions of quarter-inch holes, and these needs are not always related to a certain legal deliverable. They may want peace of mind. They may want a problem to be solved. They may want to understand their situation clearly.

Also, people may "hire" a product or service to do a "job" that's different than its seller originally intended. For example, when McDonald's wanted to sell more milkshakes, they asked their customers what they wanted in a milkshake and what might make it better. They acted on those recommendations, but giving customers what they said they wanted didn't work— McDonald's saw very little improvement in sales. So Clayton suggested that, rather than *asking* people what they wanted, the R&D group should spend some time *observing* what happened when customers bought milkshakes, so that they could look for patterns, and then dig in from there if needed. Researchers, including Clayton's colleague Gerald Berstell, spent time in various McDonald's locations, watching for when people bought milkshakes, whether they were alone or in a group, etc., and they found that most milkshakes were sold early in the morning, and most people just drove off with them.

Gerald couldn't figure out why people were buying milkshakes so early in the morning at first, but speaking to several customers and probing into what exactly they were doing with their milkshakes, the researchers discovered that people were bored on their long drive to work and needed something to do. They were also a little hungry but not hungry enough for a full meal. A milkshake did the trick. Gerald suggested a few changes, including making the milkshakes thicker so that they lasted for an entire commute and placing a milkshake dispensing machine on the other side of the retail counter with a mechanism that allowed customers to pay quickly, so they could grab their milkshake fast and be on their way to work. When McDonald's improved their delivery of milkshakes in this way, sales increased by seven times. Their product better matched the customer's job to be done.

Getting to the heart of what your clients really want—not just what they say they want—is crucial for growth at your law firm. If a client wants peace of mind from knowing that everything will be taken care of, focus on making sure they understand the process and what's going to happen. But if they want to feel supported while making emotional decisions about who gets their kids if they die, a comfortable environment and empathetic bedside manner might be more important. Focusing your efforts in the right places ensures you deliver an excellent experience that leads to more reviews, referrals, and new business.

Giving Your Clients What They Want

When a client comes to your firm, they have a problem they're hoping you can fix—a job they're hoping you can do. What they're looking for is almost certainly more nuanced than

straight-up legal advice, but it also isn't incredibly complicated. Your clients want an effortless experience, just like the
ones they receive elsewhere in their lives. This means you
need to get a sense of the reason underlying why someone
came to you in the first place and a sense of how they expect
their experience with your firm to play out.

For example, if a company hires your firm for a specific
piece of legal work, do they want the job to be handled intri-
cately and carefully, no matter how long it takes, or is speed
more important? Are they looking for frank feedback as
needed throughout the matter, or is it important to have clear,
consistent communication so that they can report progress to
board members or other key stakeholders?

If there's an expectation your clients don't even know they
have, and that they didn't think could be met when working
with a lawyer, you can provide something new that clients
find immense value in. With a bit of client-centered thinking,
you can come up with a path that benefits your law firm too.

Nicholas Hite, a lawyer in New Orleans, Louisiana, often
works with clients in the LGBTQ+ community and with sur-
vivors of intimate abuse. He's found that for people dealing
with emotionally charged situations in which they haven't had
a lot of control, it's important to feel informed and empowered throughout the legal process.

But, as a lawyer who'd just opened up his own small firm,
Nicholas didn't have the bandwidth to provide constant
updates to the 100-plus clients he was handling at any given
time. So, Nicholas thought of another way. He gives his clients access to their documents, communications, and other
case information via Clio Connect, Clio's secure communication portal. And his clients love it.

"I tell them, 'You're going to get an email, and it's going to give you access to essentially everything that I have for your file,'" Nicholas says. "'It's all right there, and you can go to it whenever you want. You don't have to wait for me to call you back or wait for me to respond to your email.' That's really empowering for my clients, that they feel that they can participate and take charge in managing their own cases. It empowers them to be really in control of the situation, so that they can go from being a victim to a survivor."

By thinking outside the box, carefully considering what his clients need, and giving them that in the most efficient way possible, Nicholas has shifted his clients' views of what a legal practice can do for them. What's beneficial for his clients is also more efficient for Nicholas: Clients wanted updates, but Nicholas recognized that he or his staff didn't have to be the ones delivering. Giving clients access to their own case information at any time minimizes the amount of follow-up and minor updating that Nicholas needs to do. In turn, this means that he's able to keep costs down. Nicholas has applied a client-centered mindset to multiple other processes at his firm, using tech to give clients what they need in a way that's efficient and cost effective. More often than not, these considerations aren't at odds—they drive each other.

By keeping his services affordable, Nicholas has opened up his firm to people who don't qualify for free legal services but who can't afford to hire a lawyer at market rates. He's accessing a new market and a ton of new clients while giving people better access to legal services. This is what it looks like to *not* put your clients first.

Nicholas began by considering what his clients would need, but he cycled his thinking outward to consider how his firm could best meet that need, and then cycled back to the center to consider how that solution would impact his clients. The result has been empowered and happy clients, a steady stream of new clients and healthy revenues, and increased access to justice in Nicholas' community.

The Power Of Being at the Center

There's one final, critical reason why I believe putting your clients at the center is the most important way for law firms to succeed in today's world: the power of human connection. Humans are social creatures with a base-level desire to fit in and be seen by other members of a group. This support is tremendously important when we're facing a significant challenge. But people don't always get the support they need, and this is especially true when they interact with companies or professional service providers.

Before Nicholas founded his firm, a number of his clients had had less-than-stellar experiences with other law firms and the legal system in general. People who are transgender entered courtrooms where their chosen names and pronouns were not used, for example. Not having your personhood considered, not having your needs considered, and not feeling seen are incredibly detrimental experiences for someone going through a legal issue that's likely one of the most difficult challenges they'll face in their lives. Minor interactions matter too: A person can feel uncared for if it takes a long time to hear back about their legal situation, or if things aren't explained in a way they can understand, or if their concerns are brushed off as unimportant. When people feel that their needs are being ignored, whether in important or seemingly inconsequential interactions, there's a level of trust that isn't given to the company, law firm, or service provider and that makes the relationship fragile. At the first opportunity, clients will choose a better experience elsewhere.

When you take the time to watch, listen, and think carefully about what it is your client truly needs and how you can get that to them, you create trust and a powerful connection that's difficult to break. Even if a client might never need to come to you again, they'll remember how you made them feel, and they'll recommend you to others.

This isn't about making grand gestures. It's about authentically caring for your clients throughout all stages of the process—and showing that through your actions. Make it easy for clients to share information before an initial consultation. Follow up in a timely manner. Know whether they'd like you to explain the options clearly and help them to make a choice, or whether they'd like you to take a more prescriptive role. It's the little things that matter.

Running a client-centered law firm isn't just another business strategy: It's a powerful mindset that puts the focus on our innate human desire to connect with others. By grounding yourself with a client-centered mindset, you'll constantly be reminded of the importance of providing a great experience and connecting with people, and you'll have a solid foundation for a profitable, successful firm. You'll continue to make decisions that turn the flywheel of success, and you'll watch your firm grow.

5

THE VALUE
OF EXPERIENCE

PROVIDING AN EFFORTLESS experience is key for meeting client expectations and succeeding in a world where those expectations have evolved. But the importance of experience goes beyond keeping your clients at the center of your thinking—the client experience is actually part of your *product*, right along with your legal services. In other words, you don't just provide a legal deliverable—you provide a legal experience.

The Commodification of Legal Services

If you're a lawyer, you know what you're doing. You went to law school. You passed the bar. You've handled difficult legal cases and understood complex aspects of the law. But unfortunately, it's difficult to compete based on your level of competence alone.

In the United States, it's extremely difficult to market yourself as a specialist or expert in any specific area of the law.

Rule 7.4 of the ABA Model Rules of Professional Conduct prohibits lawyers from stating (or even implying) that they're a specialist in a certain field of law, unless they've been formally certified as a specialist by an approved organization in their state. If you're an employment lawyer, you can say that you handle wrongful termination cases, but you can't say that you're a specialist in that area or that you're the best at it. You also can't state that you're the "best" lawyer in a certain area, unless there's a third party endorsing you.

Potential clients will ask their friends and family for a good lawyer, and then they'll look you up online to see if working with you seems as though it will be a good experience. Depending on your practice area, your clients may not know much about what it's like to work with a law firm. To them, one family law firm, real estate firm, or wills and estates lawyer is the same as the next, and an easy to navigate website and/or reviews from other clients are what help them decide who to choose. In today's world, great service, a straightforward experience, and great reviews might be the most important things that differentiate your firm from the competition.

Sometimes clients are looking to be represented by the best of the best, or to receive amazing legal advice for their complex problems. But most of the time, they want to get the job done in the simplest and most affordable way.

As we've discussed, resolving a legal matter—no matter how small—used to mean working with a lawyer, which, in many cases, was a frustrating experience. But today consumers and businesses alike are turning elsewhere, choosing new types of providers. This doesn't mean the end of law firms.

Not by a long shot. But we are at a tipping point. Law firms have a tremendous opportunity to differentiate themselves by providing better overall experiences for their clients. Better customization and more guidance through the legal process is worth a lot to clients, even for simple matters. There's currently a mismatch between what clients need and what law firms provide. To succeed in an era where there are plenty of alternatives for the delivery of legal services— and when clients are accustomed to instant service and satisfaction in other consumer interactions—law firms need to pay close attention to the experience they provide.

Experience as a Product

Many companies succeed because they think of the customer experience as a key piece of the product they sell, using that to differentiate themselves from the competition. This is especially important where a product or service is highly fungible and the difference between competing providers isn't always discernible—for example, with shoe stores and coffee shops.

Zappos was founded as an online shoe retailer in 1999, but CEO Tony Hsieh never thought of Zappos as a shoe company; he instead frames Zappos as a *service company* that happens to sell shoes. From the beginning, Zappos employees have been encouraged to go above and beyond for customers. There are no call scripts and there's no pressure to wrap up calls quickly in the customer service center at Zappos. Rather, employees are encouraged to do whatever is needed to connect with the person on the other end of the phone and provide excellent service—they even have the authority to offer refunds, pay for damages, or take other actions they deem necessary. For example, when one woman called to return boots for her father who had recently passed away, the Zappos employee she spoke to told her not to worry about returning the boots, provided a refund anyway, and sent her flowers. Zappos went above and beyond what those who wrote *The Effortless Experience* would recommend, but the point here is that Tony Hsieh is *very* aware of how much the customer experience intertwines with his product, and he leverages that however he can. This approach led to 75% of Zappos sales coming from repeat customers and to Zappos being acquired by Amazon for $1.2 billion in 2009. To be clear, Zappos doesn't throw caution to the wind when providing these excellent service experiences: It took a strategic approach of spending less on marketing so that it could spend more on customer experience.

And it isn't a customer-first company. It's customer-centered, and it looks out for its employees too. A significant part of Zappos' success is often attributed to the amazing internal culture that the company has built, in part by heavily reinforcing its values. (Zappos offers $3,000 to quit the day your initial training concludes, based on the theory that if you take the money, you're not a fit for the company anyway.)

Starbucks is another company that has built its reputation on experiences. The founders of Starbucks were inspired by Italian café culture, and Howard Schultz opened the first Seattle coffee shop to serve espresso beverages and offer the relaxed atmosphere of an Italian café. As the company has grown, Starbucks has maintained its focus on creating a welcoming, positive atmosphere for customers. All over the world, the look and feel of a Starbucks, and the taste of a Starbucks beverage, is consistent (with maybe a few local touches). Starbucks says that its work is "really about human connection," and it walks the talk: When one customer wrote in to say that they felt unwelcome when their local Starbucks started putting away outside chairs and tables 30 minutes ahead of closing, the store responded within 24 hours and began leaving the chairs out until closing.

Like Zappos, Starbucks is also customer-centered, not customer-first. It treats its employees extremely well: Early in the company's history, Starbucks began offering full health benefits to eligible full- and part-time employees. Starbucks also calls its employees "partners" and offers them stock options to create a sense of shared ownership at the company.

Both Zappos and Starbucks focus on providing an amazing customer experience *and* an amazing environment for their employees, and doing so has allowed them to transform otherwise unassuming commodities into stand-out experiences and powerful brands.

Unless you're after a pair of red-soled Christian Louboutin heels, or a famed $1,000 cup of coffee, a pair of heels and a cup of joe are pretty much the same wherever you go. Zappos and Starbucks sell products that most anyone would be able to sell, but they offer an experience that few others are willing to match—and that's made all the difference.

The same goes for law firms: Beyond a certain base level of competency that lawyers are required by ethics rules to meet, most legal deliverables are interchangeable. Your ability to differentiate yourself from the competition based on your work product alone is likely limited; however, you have virtually unlimited opportunity to differentiate yourself based on the client experience you provide.

" ——

Your ability to differentiate yourself from the competition based on your work product alone is likely limited; however, you have virtually unlimited opportunity to differentiate yourself based on the client experience you provide.

—— "

Legal Deliverable + Legal Experience = One Product

A legal deliverable and/or advice is the core, concrete "product" you provide. This is table stakes, and many other law firms can provide a similar product. But you can add an additional layer of value around that core deliverable that gets bigger and richer the more attuned you are to every experience your client has with your firm. Conversely, if these experiences are actively negative, the value a client sees in your legal deliverable diminishes.

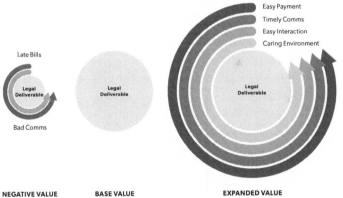

HOW BIG IS THE VALUE OF YOUR LEGAL PRODUCT?

You don't provide a legal service, you deliver a legal product. The value of that product is the sum of the value your client gets from your legal deliverable *and* their legal experience.

Jess Birken, a nonprofit lawyer in Minneapolis, Minnesota, is highly conscious of how the experience she provides intertwines with her legal services to create a standout product for her clients. The website for Birken Law is extremely clear and easy to navigate: Visit it, and you'll quickly see where to learn about Jess, schedule a consultation, or pay an invoice. This streamlined experience alone puts Jess' firm a cut above most others, but she goes even further to provide a positive experience for her clients: Jess creates a relaxed environment that helps her nonprofit clients feel at ease. You're more likely to find her in a striped T-shirt than a collared shirt, and clients know what to expect because this is obvious when you visit her website. If a client wants a formal big-law experience, they wouldn't go to Jess—they'd go to a larger firm with a more buttoned-up culture. If a client wants a form filled out, they'd go to a document filing service.

In each case, the client is getting a certain legal deliverable, but it's being delivered in different ways, and each case constitutes a very different product. As Jess puts it, "When my clients hire me, they're not just hiring me to produce the work. They're hiring the experience. They're hiring the sense of security. They're hiring the relationship."

The experience your firm creates adds an extra layer around your legal services—it can increase the total value of the service you provide and can open up a world of possible options to help your firm stand out. Fail to provide a good client experience, and you'll have a tough time competing—your firm will provide no greater value than your competition. At the heart of this, it's important not to lose sight of what it means to run a client-centered law firm: knowing what your clients want, and giving that to them in the simplest way possible.

Your Clients Don't Want a Will

You can put a price on a will, but you can't put a price on the security of knowing your children are protected.

My wife and I have had wills made at two points in our lives: once before we had children and once afterward. Most recently, we had a will drawn up by Jason Golbey at Golbey Law. From the start, it was clear that Jason had put a lot of thought and effort into creating experiences that made sense for his clients. He knew exactly what kind of interactions we would like and what made sense to us. Our first interaction was an in-person meeting where we spent a lot of time talking about why we wanted a will, what was most important to us, and how he would work with us to help make that a reality. From then on out, a lot of the process was handled electronically. We communicated and reviewed documents online, and we used e-signatures when we signed our engagement letter. Compared with our previous experience making a will, the whole thing was a piece of cake.

Creating our first will, before Clio was launched and before my wife and I had children, was a much heavier experience. There were multiple visits, wet signatures were always required, and our documents all needed to be couriered. The difference was night and day. If I had the choice, I would choose an experience like the one Jason provided each and every time. Wills themselves are fairly commodified. That's not really what we were buying from our lawyer: We were buying a sense of security.

Legal clients who walk in asking for a will are not simply looking for a crisp new document to grace their safety deposit box. They want to know that their children (or other

Wills themselves are fairly commodified. That's not really what we were buying from our lawyer: We were buying a sense of security.

dependents) will be taken care of if something happens to them, and that assurance comes from how the process is handled, how at ease the client feels, and how well the contents of the will and how to use it are explained to them.

Mastercard's famous multi-decade "priceless" advertising campaign highlights the value of the experiences we spend money on and the real reason that we're buying certain products or services. It's clear why this campaign has resonated with audiences for so long: You can put a price on a will, but you can't put a price on the security of knowing your children are protected. You can put a price on an incorporation, but you can't put a price on the joy of striking out on your own and knowing everything is in good order. That's how much value you provide through the legal experience. The legal deliverable your clients hire you for is a means to an end, but the legal experience—the way you handle the process of *getting* them that legal deliverable—is what can leave them satisfied.

Thinking of experience as part of what you sell is a critical shift: Experience is part and parcel of the product you sell, right alongside any legal deliverables, and you can create a high-value moat that differentiates your firm from competitors. Ignore the value of the legal experience, and you risk losing clients to other firms and services who *are* willing to invest in it.

The Elements of a Good Legal Experience

A big part of giving your clients what they want is what I've been talking about for most of this chapter: providing a good client experience. What does a good experience look like? In true lawyer fashion, the answer is "it depends," since every practice area, location, client, and issue is different. But there are two universal aspects that every law firm should keep in mind:

1. Building trust
2. Minimizing friction

These aspects are heavily intertwined: A frictionless experience helps build trust, while a strong level of trust in the relationship means interactions between your client and firm run far more smoothly. If you can build a relationship and a certain level of trust with your clients—one that goes beyond the base level of trust they have in you as a licensed professional—you'll be ahead of plenty of other firms and position your practice to succeed.

Building Trust

You work with the law every day. Depending on your area of practice, you may also be regularly exposed to incredibly difficult situations with people going through the worst experiences of their lives. It's tough, no doubt, but it's your day-to-day, and you know what to expect. For your clients, who don't live what you live every day, and who may even be "legal beginners," it's a whole different ball game. They don't know what they don't know, and they need to trust that you can get them through it.

Imagine an expert skier, let's call her Sally, approaching a difficult, steep black-diamond run on her favorite mountain. She's heard that it snowed overnight, and she's excited to cruise through some fresh snow, but as she starts heading down the run, it becomes clear that many other skiers had the same idea. The fresh snow is gone, replaced by large, icy moguls. Sally is a bit disappointed, but it's okay: She's been in this situation before, and she knows how to take her time, adjust her style, and get down the run confidently.

Now imagine that Sally isn't alone. She's brought her friend Maggie along, and Maggie is a beginner skier. She's keen, but she's never attempted a black-diamond run in her life, and she's terrified of the run, fresh snow or not. For Maggie, the run is definitely not as straightforward as it is for Sally. If Sally carefully and patiently coaches Maggie down the run by encouraging her, telling her about rocks or steeper sections to watch out for, and explaining how to stay in control, she'll build trust with her and they'll have a good experience. Maggie will likely still be terrified, but she'll also feel excited that she's completed her first black-diamond run ever.

But if Sally snaps at Maggie, doesn't answer questions she has about how to approach the run, and disregards her fear and anxiety, Maggie will end up feeling frustrated and angry at Sally for insisting they try a black-diamond run. She won't remember the experience fondly (or recommend going skiing with Sally to her friends).

Facing a legal issue is new or at least unfamiliar territory for most people. Clients need to trust that you are competent and can give them the legal deliverable they need, but they also need to trust that the whole experience will be as painless as possible. They need to know that they'll be supported, that their questions will be answered, and that you'll ensure they have an accurate understanding of their options and how their legal matter will be handled.

It's incredibly hard to build trust with clients, but doing so builds goodwill. Things will run more smoothly for your law firm, because clients will be more inclined to give you the benefit of the doubt when things go wrong. If you focus on providing a great end-to-end experience, and you slip up one time (say, you send your bills a little too late, or you're having a bad day and take a frustrated tone with your client), that base level of trust you've already built with your client will help bridge the gap to solve the problem.

For example, I love Amazon and use it frequently. Once upon a time, I had an experience that disappointed me, but Amazon was quick to rectify it, leaving me with even more faith in the brand than I'd had before. I'd ordered a bike rack on a Monday for a trip on the upcoming weekend and had selected a shipping option that would ensure the bike arrived by Friday. But when I looked at how the shipment was tracking on Wednesday, it showed as not arriving until the following week. I was disappointed. I wrote to Amazon to let them know that this delay meant my family would need to cancel our biking trip. They were apologetic and offered me a free month of Amazon Prime as compensation. That was a nice gesture, but it wasn't something I cared about, and I let Amazon know as much. To be clear, at this point, I'd accepted the outcome and wasn't expecting anything further from Amazon—I simply wanted to share my feedback.

But Amazon didn't settle with me feeling lukewarm about the experience and went above and beyond to rectify the situation: They credited me the entire cost of the bike rack! I was blown away. And the kicker was the rack showed up on Friday anyway. Based on that experience, my trust in Amazon was strengthened, and I'll continue to buy from them for the foreseeable future—but I'm not sure my feeling would be the same if I'd been ordering from a company that hadn't previously given me many incredible, customer-centered experiences. To build trust, you've got to provide great experiences consistently.

Build a strong relationship, and you'll get a second chance with clients when you slip up. Conversely, if you haven't built trust, and your client is already on edge waiting for updates or anxiously questioning every piece of advice or information you share, adding a minor slip-up to the mix could be the straw that breaks the proverbial camel's back. It will be much harder to resolve the issue to the client's satisfaction, so you could lose the client, and be at risk of receiving negative reviews.

Focus on building trust and understanding what your client needs from the outset, and you'll provide more value and help the case move along smoothly for your law firm as well.

Minimizing Friction

When I'm in the market for a service provider, whether a law firm or otherwise, one of the key things I look for is how committed the provider is to minimizing friction throughout my experience. I'll do a bit of research, but once I've narrowed it down to a number of options with a four-star rating or higher, I'll make my choice based on who's going to be the easiest to deal with. The reality for me is that life happens in the three minutes I get between meetings. I don't have the time to listen to a voicemail and call someone back: I need a quick update via email or text.

And I'm not alone. There's a story I love to tell about a long-tenured staff member at Clio and how he chose his dentist: After looking at a few decently rated options, he made his

Focus on building trust and understanding what your client needs from the outset, and you'll provide more value and help the case move along smoothly for your law firm as well.

decision based on which dentist would let him book appointments via a website, because he absolutely did *not* want to have to call in for an appointment. Modern life is busy, and people need the administrative aspects of life to be dealt with as efficiently as possible. Couple that with the expectation for every interaction to be an Amazon-like experience, and the case for investing in frictionless client experiences is clear.

People phoned back and forth to schedule their appointments 15 years ago, because that was the best option. But today, there are much *better* options. You can schedule an appointment via text, email, or online scheduling tool. And while potential clients may not set out to find a lawyer who specifically lets you book online, they will absolutely choose their law firm based on how easy it would be to work with them.

Think about restaurants, for example. Almost everyone I know used to be fine with calling a restaurant to reserve a table. But today, they'll choose a restaurant based on what they can reserve online via OpenTable, Yelp, or other similar apps. Sure, if it's a special night and they're trying to get a table at the best restaurant in town, they'll call, but that situation isn't reflective of most people's needs most of the time.

I'll include one important interjection about technology here: Tech can absolutely help you minimize friction for your clients: Beyond scheduling software, there are tools that will send automatic case updates to clients, tools that make it easy for clients to input information and tell you about their case, and tools that keep client information consolidated and organized so you don't need to ask them the same questions over and over. But providing a frictionless experience doesn't always have to be about tech, and the systems and processes you implement at your firm definitely shouldn't be *driven* by shiny new tech. The main thing is to be in tune with your clients' needs and to deliver the experience they're looking for in a way that makes sense to them.

Providing a Consistent Product

When you minimize friction and build trust with your clients, things flow smoothly, your clients aren't anxiously wondering what is happening with their case, and when all is said and done, they feel like they got what they needed. But this type of experience must be provided consistently. Your clients need to trust that they *will* have a low-friction experience, and their expectations must continue to be met, or your firm risks losing their trust.

Imagine a client who starts working with a law firm and, after their initial consultation, communicates mainly via text. This works for them, and they're pleased the firm adopted this option and understands their lifestyle. But one day, someone at the firm calls the client about a trivial matter related to their case, leaves a voicemail when they don't pick up, and asks them to call back. The client is a bit thrown. "I thought they got me," they think. "I thought they understood what worked for me. Maybe I was wrong? If they're not getting this, what *else* are they missing?" In this case, a small amount of trust was lost, and the firm will need to earn that back.

Conversely, you can also provide a positive experience in an unfortunate situation to help build a client's trust. I had one such experience with Uber. A few years ago, I had an Uber ride "stolen." I ordered an Uber, but when the car arrived, someone else got in, and the car drove off. Needless to say, I was left without a ride, frustrated and annoyed. I wanted to make sure I wasn't about to be charged for a ride I didn't take. However, my frustration quickly subsided after Uber swiftly dealt with the issue. I emailed Uber to let them know what had happened, and in just a few minutes, I had a reply in my inbox confirming a refund for the trip. Dealing with this unexpected inconvenience was a very low friction, low effort experience, and it met my expectations. I only had to email the company once, and my concerns were dealt with quickly. This shouldn't have been a surprise based on my previous interactions with Uber, but the exchange colored my unfortunate experience in a more positive light, and it left me with an elevated feeling of trust in the company, knowing that if things went a little sideways, they'd have my back.

For your legal clients, this feeling of trust is even more powerful. In a situation where your client may feel like they don't have a lot of control, it's important for them to have an advocate and expert they can trust. And if they're not getting that feeling from you, they'll look to get it from someone else.

Consistently embrace all aspects of the client experience as part of the product you provide, and you'll build lasting relationships with clients who will keep coming back to and/or referring business to your firm. With this approach, you'll position your firm to succeed even as client expectations continue to evolve.

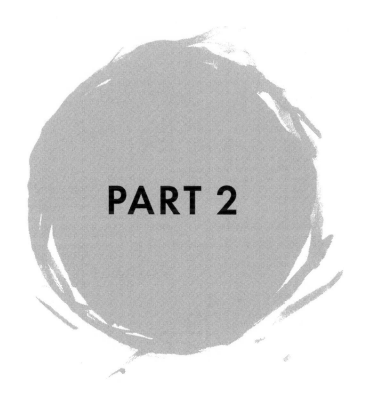

PART 2

6

THE CLIENT-CENTERED LAW FIRM

IN PART 1, we explored the sea change being experienced by the legal industry and established that to meet evolving client expectations, lawyers and legal professionals must let go of the traditional law firm business model and adopt a client-centered mindset. Your clients will be at the center—the core of your law firm—while the firm and the legal services it provides make up a protective outer layer. Decisions about process and tech should cycle between the center and the outer layer to consider both law firm and client.

So what exactly does a client-centered law firm look like?

The Five Values of a Client-Centered Law Firm

Every client-centered law firm will operate differently. There's no list of steps with clear instructions to follow, because what it means to run a client-centered law firm will vary for every lawyer and every practice. Being client-centered means a commitment to your clients, a recognition that the client experience goes beyond legal representation, and an understanding that your firm needs to run efficiently and have a positive culture to provide a good client experience.

It's easy to believe you're a client-centered law firm, but it's much more challenging to stay intensely curious about what it is your clients *actually* need, look at how you might give that to them, and cycle decisions between the inner client core and outer law firm layer. The following five values provide a framework to think about what it means to be a client-centered firm. These might show up in your mission statement, but when they're really lived out day-to-day, you'll find yourself running a client-centered firm.

1. Develop Deep Client Empathy

When your clients are facing challenges, no doubt you feel some level of sympathy toward them. But having empathy is different: It helps you understand your client and ensure they feel heard. Empathy empowers you to design better client experiences, and it can also help you diffuse a stressful situation. Your instinct might be to keep a thick layer of emotional armor on when dealing with a stressed client, but, as health psychologist and Stanford University lecturer Kelly McGonigal says, it's better to let their stress be a little bit contagious. Being truly open and empathetic—rather than nodding and acknowledging their situation but still keeping your guard up—helps your clients feel heard and calms them. Opening up also clarifies your own goals so you can better address the situation.

You may be drafting your fourth will of the week, but your client has never had a will made before. You might be helping out your tenth immigration client for the month, but this is the one and only time that client will immigrate to the United States. If you can combine your expertise with deep empathy for your clients' experiences, you'll be better positioned to create a more painless legal experience for them.

To cultivate empathy, put yourself in your clients' shoes as much as you can. Think about how you would feel if you were having their legal experience. Would you feel satisfied? Or frustrated? Even better, go through the same processes you put your clients through. Google "divorce lawyer in Tennessee," for example, and see if your firm shows up. Try filling out your website contact form on your phone when you're in line at the bank. Send yourself an invoice and walk through what it takes to pay it.

Note that cultivating empathy is different from simply thinking about your client's situation: You need to think about who they are as a person. **You are not your client.** Your client might come from a different socioeconomic background from you. They might have low vision or low hearing. Is your intake form easy to fill out for someone with dexterity issues? If you're not sure what it's like to be your client, or if you're curious about a specific aspect of their experience, just ask the question—there might be a learning opportunity for you.

2. Practice Attentiveness

Have you ever reached out to someone about a problem you're having, and the person assumed they knew how to solve it— before they'd even become clear on the issue? Or have you talked to a person and had the distinct impression they were just waiting for you to finish, so they could talk? Those behaviors don't create a strong basis for a relationship. If you jump to conclusions about what your client wants from you, you risk getting it wrong and providing a legal experience (and potentially a legal deliverable) that leaves them feeling anything but relieved.

Prioritize listening, asking questions, and demonstrating understanding until you have a clear idea of what your client is looking for. Reflective listening is a helpful practice. Confirm your understanding by repeating what you're hearing back to them. The important thing is to give your clients your full attention.

People can sense a lack of attentiveness, and when you first start practicing this, you are likely to find your mind wandering to potential solutions, or you'll notice you've stopped listening and are waiting for the client to finish speaking so that you can say your piece. The more you practice attentiveness, the easier it will become to sustain. Listen well and build a strong foundation of trust.

3. Generate Ease With Communication

Clear and open communication is absolutely critical to the success of any client-centered law firm. In fact, if you're not communicating effectively, you're taking a big risk: At the time of writing, communication errors made up more than 40% of LAWPRO claims for most practice areas.

If you can proactively give a client regular updates on their case or issue, they'll feel valued, and they'll feel at ease, which means less time spent on inbound calls asking for updates for both your client *and* your firm.

Think about what your default tempo of communication is. For example, if you're representing a business undergoing a major transaction, it might make sense to provide a daily update on how things are progressing, even if the only update you have is that you haven't yet heard anything back from the other party on the documents you've sent them to review. Open communication also might just mean giving clients the ability to access case information themselves, like Nicholas Hite did with the Clio Connect client portal in Chapter 4.

The important things to think about are:

- What your clients need or want to know.
- How to say it in a way that makes sense to them.

Let's say your client has never used a lawyer before. They're nervous, they're apprehensive, and they don't know what they don't know. Don't leave it to your clients to ask the right questions about their case: Instead, be on the lookout for missing information, and don't be afraid to ask lots of questions to ensure you have all of the details you need and they understand the process. Make it clear how they can reach you if they think of something else, and lay out specific next steps. Tell your clients that you *expect* them to reach out if they have a question.

If you get the same questions over and over from new clients, consider putting together a FAQ to make sure these questions are answered quickly and easily. Also, lose the legal jargon when talking to clients. Explain issues and answer questions in terms your clients can understand, and you'll save yourself and your clients a lot of grief.

Overall, generating ease through communication means defaulting to clarity and transparency. As you start to develop deep empathy for your clients, you'll understand why it's critical for them to be proactively and regularly informed about what's going on with their case—and not be caught off guard.

4. Demand Effortless Experiences

Giving clients what they truly need means making their legal experience as easy and effortless as possible. But as we've discussed, there's no need to go over the top. Conversely, it's important not to slip into doing whatever's easiest for your law firm without considering your clients. Being client-centered means staying focused on what type of experience your clients *actually* want and need and treating that as your north star.

Asking your client to fax you something (or receive a fax), fill out forms by hand, or come to your office multiple times during their working hours to sign documents requires a lot of effort on their part. Simple changes like sharing documents electronically, and allowing e-signatures, make for a much smoother experience. The best part is, creating an effortless experience for your clients often means creating an effortless experience for your firm too. The improved processes and efficiencies mean less rote work.

It doesn't have to happen all at once. It's better to implement small, continuous, iterative changes than it is to implement nothing at all. Creating an effortless experience for your clients doesn't mean taking on a monolithic two-year project before you see any results. Small changes have a big impact, and over time, there's a cumulative positive effect. The more you can make small changes, learn, and iterate on them, the closer you'll get to providing the type of experience your clients want and need.

"

___

Being client-centered means staying focused on what type of experience your clients actually want and need and treating that as your north star.

___

"

THE LAW FIRM FLYWHEEL

5. Create Clients For Life

The legal experience should be a partnership where you work with and empower your client throughout and beyond your initial engagement. This one is simpler than you think. Consider: Do you tell your clients what to do? Or do you give them options and let them choose? Do you consider your clients to have a seat at the table in firm-wide meetings, as Jeff Bezos famously does? Or do you forget about them at the door? Do you collaborate with your clients?

Building a client-centered law firm means bringing clients *into* conversations so that you can work on problems together. You may be an expert in the law, but those outside of law bring valuable insight to the table. Treating your clients as partners puts them in a position to guide you toward providing the type of service modern legal clients want in the experience-driven era.

Likely, you'll also find that when you talk to your clients more, you'll get more business. A friend recently said to me that they've never worked with a lawyer that reasonably expected them to be a repeat customer, even though it would be very easy to create that relationship. Wills need to be updated. People get divorced more than once. Businesses require the expertise of a lawyer more than once. I'm not saying every new client you have will be opening up a new matter every month, but there's a long game you can play that benefits both your firm and your clients: Your firm needs more business, and your clients need to feel at ease when it comes to their legal matters. It's win-win.

Think Outside the Billable Hour

Translating the values of a client-centered law firm into innovative ideas that improve the day-to-day experiences of both your clients and your staff requires diligently cultivating an ongoing curiosity and openness. This may lead you to look at alternatives to established processes, or traditional business models. Take the pricing of legal services by the hour, for example. In the traditional law firm model, clients agree to pay for an undetermined number of hours at the outset of a case, potentially with little to no indication of what the final cost will be. Lawyers have plenty of data on hand that could help them estimate a final cost—at the very least, they have more information than their legal clients do—and a tiny bit of risk in estimating would make for an immensely better client experience. Yet, lawyers still ask clients to shoulder the majority of the risk.

This issue has been written about by many in the legal industry, but one of my favorite examples used to illustrate the problem comes from Ed Walters of Fastcase. Imagine going to a fancy restaurant and ordering lobster. When you ask how much it is going to cost, your server tells you that the price will need to account for the fisherman's time, the time the truck driver needs to deliver the lobster to the restaurant, and the time the chef needs to prepare the lobster. He can't tell you how much it will be until you get your check at the end of the meal. Would you order that lobster?

There's a reason most restaurants don't make their customers wait to see the final price: It's fairly easy for them to estimate what the final cost will be, because they have the most data on hand and the most experience when it comes to serving lobster at restaurants, and providing the cost up-front creates a better customer experience. Restaurant goers can enjoy their meal without worrying about what the final cost will be, because the restaurant has created an effortless experience for them. But law firms don't do this, and it creates a terrible client experience. There are better ways.

Charging flat fees where possible is one of them. Lawyers may offer bespoke legal advice, but for certain types of legal deliverables, it's entirely possible to set a fixed fee based on an estimated cost for the piece of work. It doesn't mean that lawyers need to be paid less for their work either. Developing deep empathy for what clients actually need would allow firms to base fees on factors like how long it normally takes to complete the work, how much overhead is involved, and, most importantly, how much value it brings to clients—getting a clear read on that last one can even help you up your prices.

Another example of a better way is the subscription model where unlimited legal advice, document review, and/ or business planning are offered in exchange for a monthly fee. Kimberly Y. Bennett, an Atlanta-based trademark and business strategy attorney, and owner of K. Bennett Law, is focused on providing better client experiences with a sub-scription model—but she's also conscious of how it benefits her firm. She no longer needs to worry about fluctuating rev-enues, because her subscription model sees a predictable revenue stream coming in each month.

Kim thought of a way for her firm to think outside the billable hour and found that a client-centered subscription service model provided more peace of mind for both her cli-ents and her firm. Prior to offering subscription legal services, Kim recalls, "The client wasn't happy, and I surely wasn't happy, so I needed to figure out a better way to work with clients that didn't depend on me saying 'my value is based on the amount of time that I'm spending with you.'" Today, legal clients want a menu and a price for their legal services.

Even the notoriously slow-to-change governing bodies of the legal industry have started to adapt to this demand for legal service providers to generate ease with communi-cation and demand effortless experiences for their clients. In December 2018, new price transparency rules came into effect for solicitors in England and Wales from the Solicitors Regulation Authority (SRA): They require that pricing infor-mation be displayed on a law firm's website, in a clear and easy to understand format, with the basis for the charges explained. Lawyers must provide a total cost for their ser-vices—and they must provide an average or a range of costs when that isn't possible.

Being client-centered means adopting a mindset that naturally leads you to the conclusion that pricing should be transparent, *before* your regulatory authority makes it a rule to get law firms to act.

Client-Centered, Tech Savvy

Technology isn't the main driver of what it means to run a client-centered law firm, but it's a critical part of it. In a world where legal consumers expect Amazon-like experiences, running a practice with a pen and a legal pad no longer cuts it.

But tech without process—and tech without a client-centered mindset to guide its use and implementation—is just another shiny tool that staff and/or clients won't use. Technology needs to fit *into* processes that are designed to provide good experiences and solve clients' problems—and you'll need to practice attentiveness to work out what those processes are. If tech doesn't fit, that's okay. The solution needs to work for *your* clients. Maybe you practice elder law and many of your clients don't have smartphones. Or maybe you serve low-income clients who have limited access to tech. Or maybe you work with people recently released from multi-decade prison sentences who don't use the latest tech. In each of these scenarios, staunchly running a digital-only law firm and giving clients the option to contact you via an app would not be demanding effortless experiences, and it definitely wouldn't reflect a client-centered approach. However, setting up internal reminders for yourself to call or text these clients with status updates *would* be effective. You simply need to meet your clients where they are, not where you think they should be.

On the other hand, if you're serving corporate clients, family law clients, or immigration clients, a more tech-savvy client-centered approach may be appropriate. Form-heavy practice areas like immigration can be automated in a way that puts the client experience first—as Greg McLawsen of Sound Immigration in Seattle has done. Sound Immigration is a decentralized, paperless, and cloud-based office that bills itself as America's online immigration firm. Attorneys work remotely, and most services are delivered online. The firm uses tools like Clio, Slack, Trello, Ruby Receptionists, and Zapier to keep things running smoothly in the background and to ensure no client ever needs to unnecessarily enter the same information twice. But it's not the automated, streamlined, cost-efficient way of doing business that sets Sound Immigration apart. It's definitely a positive that the business runs smoothly and efficiently, but there are plenty of other companies out there trying to completely automate the service.

What sets the firm apart is the client experience it provides. Above all else, Sound Immigration has developed deep client empathy and works hard to generate ease with communication. Going through the immigration process can be nerve-racking to say the least. When someone is six months into the process, worried about their future, about getting naturalized, or about getting to stay in the US with their family, they want to know that everything is going to be okay—and knowing where their case is in the process can help with that. Sound Immigration empathetically addresses this need by allowing clients the ability to book a 15-minute call online. This call is free of charge, so clients can rest easy when it comes to cost. This service, which keeps communication open, is part of the biggest value-add Greg believes Sound Immigration provides on top of its legal services: getting the human side of legal services right.

Tech doesn't make Sound Immigration client-centered: Sound Immigration *leverages* technology to run efficiently and enable client-centered processes. The 15-minute consultation is only possible because the firm uses an online system to help clients book time with lawyers, even though they're all in different locations. Furthermore, administrative processes run efficiently in the background, which allows lawyers to devote more focus and energy toward counseling their clients through the immigration process. Tech is always going to be useful in the backend of your law firm, freeing up time that you can invest elsewhere. A good accounting system, appointment booking system, payment system, and so on are the building blocks for your firm's back office.

In every case, it's critical to make sure you've got the right tool for both your firm *and* your clients. This is another subject that Greg feels strongly about: A major pain point for both him and his clients is the transfer of information needed for immigration forms from client to attorney. When he initially started looking for a better solution, there were plenty of programs on the market, but none of them would have provided a good client experience. One of the platforms would have required questionnaires to be sent in two stints rather than all at once—that meant instead of clients setting aside a chunk of time to get all their information together and fill out all necessary forms in one go, they would have received a surprise second round of questions.

As Greg says, that would have sucked from the client perspective. It's always worth it to demand effortless experiences for clients, and that's what Greg did. It took six to eight years from when he started looking for a platform that would minimize client pain until he found one, but he held out until he got something that truly served his clients' needs.

There's one more thing: The way Greg has set up Sound Immigration allows him to travel for several months every year. He uses cloud-based programs so that he can access his practice from anywhere, uses a virtual receptionist service to ensure no call goes unanswered, and automates what he can to minimize the time he needs to spend in front of the computer while in Thailand, Bhutan, or India. Who doesn't want the freedom to travel several months per year?

With the right tech implemented the right way, the possibilities are endless for how you can provide a better client experience, run a more efficient law firm, and work in a way that better fits your lifestyle too.

Cultivating a Client-Centered Mindset

Meaningful change takes a lot of effort, but it's invaluable once achieved. Law firms have been structured one way for a very long time, and moving toward a client-centered mindset won't happen overnight. It will be a slow, sustained effort that involves choosing to put clients at the center every day. There won't be a finish line to cross either.

What it means to be a client-centered law firm is constantly changing, and that change will continue as law firms, businesses, and consumer expectations evolve. The values of developing deep client empathy, practicing attentiveness, generating ease with communication, demanding effortless experiences, and creating clients for life are the guiding principles—and as the world innovates, and people's daily experiences shift, the ways those values manifest in practical terms will continue to change.

For this reason, it's important to adopt a client-centered *mindset*, rather than any sort of rigid client-centered *model*. In her book *Mindset*, Stanford University psychologist Carol Dweck discusses the differences between fixed and growth mindsets. People who have a fixed mindset believe that their abilities are, well, fixed, and they don't have much control over them. This leads to a fear of failure and pessimism in the face of failure. People with a growth mindset, on the other hand, cultivate a passion for learning new things and cultivating new qualities. They embrace failure as a learning opportunity. The growth mindset is where law firms need to be. Building a client-centered law firm is a process, and failure is okay.

Of course, I'm not asking you to be reckless and take risks that could lead to a malpractice suit. But a failed initiative to get clients to text instead of call, or a failed implementation of a client portal that no one adopts, are examples of failures you might encounter. You will probably get it wrong. You might introduce a new process only to find out clients hate it. You might even find that clients are resistant to you trying to provide a better level of service and experience for them, because they've been so used to doing it the old way. You might decide you want to lead the charge for client-centered innovation at your firm, and your first proposal might get rejected. And that's all okay.

At the end of the day, what matters is whether *you* decide to go back to the old way, because it's familiar—or whether you decide to push forward, learn from small failures, and grow a client-centered law firm to succeed in the 21st century.

7

EXPERIENCING YOUR LAW FIRM

WHAT'S IT LIKE to work with your law firm, from a client's point of view? To answer that question, think about their entire legal experience. It doesn't start when you're officially retained: From your client's point of view, their legal experience extends from when they first realize they have a problem and start looking for a lawyer to well after the final bill is paid, when a friend or colleague asks if they'd recommend your firm.

In more general business terms, this is what's called the client journey. Looking at the client experience in terms of a journey means thinking explicitly about the different phases a client goes through when they're getting a legal need met, and what their practical and emotional wants and needs are during each phase. It's important to note that the client journey is made up of interactions from your *client's* point of view. You won't be interacting with them directly during every stage of their experience—your staff, the tools you use, and even the way you advertise your firm play a part.

A client's journey starts even before you first speak with them—once they realize they have a legal issue and start looking for help, their first point of contact with your firm is your firm's ad, a referral from a friend, or a listing in a directory. If the experience of finding you, learning about you, and contacting you is difficult, that only colors their experience negatively later on—or worse, it could be enough to stop them considering you at all. Similarly, the client's experience at the end of the journey is also extremely important. If they receive a bill that's unclear, lacking in detail, or with a much higher total than they expected, that's going to cast a negative tone over their earlier experience with you. They'll have a similarly unpleasant experience if they're forced to use an inconvenient and time-consuming method to pay their bill, i.e., via check.

The full client journey matters. In order to build a client-centered law firm, you need empathy for your clients at every stage of the journey in order to create an experience they'll actually want.

A Tale of Two Law Firms

Imagine an older loved one is sick. They've had numerous health challenges, but mentally they're still there. Suddenly, they take a turn for the worse, and their doctor tells you they have days to live. That's when you find out: They have no will.

Your loved one never got around to making one, and now they're extremely anxious, convinced they're going to leave a mess behind for their family. You calm them and resolve to get a will made quickly. You frantically search for a lawyer

66 _____

The full client journey matters. In order to build a client-centered law firm, you need empathy for your clients at every stage of the journey in order to create an experience they'll actually want.

_____ 99

and find a few in your area online with decent reviews, but it's difficult to find contact information on their sites.

Finally you get someone on the phone and tell them about your emergency. The first person you speak to tells you it's impossible to create a will that quickly and hangs up with zero questions or consideration about what you're going through. You fill out a "contact us" form for another firm, providing plenty of detail about the situation and making it clear you need help right away, but a day passes with no response, so you try to find another firm.

You reach someone who's willing to help you but only begrudgingly. In every interaction, they repeat that your loved one should have created their will earlier, and that it will be very difficult to quickly create a will at this stage. You look up "testamentary capacity" yourself, because the lawyer says it's important but you're not *really* sure how this impacts the will. Your loved one gets progressively more anxious as the lawyer asks them questions and afterward tells you they felt pressured to make decisions on the spot and aren't positive that what they said was right. In the end, you get a completed will, which is a relief, but you're not exactly sure what to do with it, and the whole experience leaves you feeling a bit off. (Later on, when the will is executed, you find that there are no issues with it and everything is in good order, but that doesn't change your impression of the experience.)

Finally, you get your bill. You're surprised that it's so high. There's very little detail, and when you call the office to ask questions, you have to ask for clarification several times before you finally feel like you have *some* understanding of the charges. Oh, and the firm only accepts payment by check—so you rummage through all your drawers trying to find the few checks you keep on hand for situations like this, can't find one, and realize you need to order checks just to pay this legal bill. What was already a difficult, sad, and stressful time for your family was made worse by the difficulty of finding a lawyer, getting a will sorted out, and even paying the bill at the end. You don't leave a review, and you definitely don't recommend the firm to others. If anything, you share the negative experience with your friends. In this case, you got what you needed, but the client experience was subpar, and in the end, that didn't lead to a positive outcome for either you (the client) or the law firm. The quality of your entire experience as a client was all but ignored, and that left you feeling anxious and unheard.

Now, imagine instead that you were the law firm in this scenario, not the client. You've just missed out on a massive opportunity to improve your firm's bottom line. (By the way, if this story resonates with you, know that you're not alone. You're in the vast majority of law firms: As we've seen in previous chapters, most firms aren't providing as good a client experience as they could be.)

With just a few small changes (many of which wouldn't cost a dime), this experience could have left the client feeling supported during a hard time, feeling clear about what the will meant and how to handle it from there, and with a full understanding of billing. Instead of the client recounting how difficult the process was, they could be telling their friends how easy you were to work with, and how their friends should really take care of the wills in their families (and your client knows just the person to do it for them).

Plenty of firms are employing innovative approaches to provide a better experience for clients throughout the whole legal process. They're making their internal processes more efficient, they're doing incredibly meaningful work, and they're doing it by making sure that every interaction with their law firm, at every stage of the client journey, matches what the client needs.

Cascade Legal Planning, a firm focused on wills and estate planning in Portland, Oregon, regularly deals with situations like the one described above. They get frantic calls from spouses or children of people who have only days to live but who have no will or medical directives—and Cascade springs into action. Cascade is easy to contact in the first place. A phone number, email, address, and an appointment booking system are all clearly visible on the home page of its website. One of the firm's lawyers meets with the client as soon as possible to determine testamentary capacity. Then an effective will is quickly drafted with the help of Clio and WealthCounsel. The office is able to quickly put a final plan together, sometimes within 24 hours, and the attorney and a notary drive to either the hospice center or the client's home to execute the estate plan. Documents are scanned into the cloud then and there to ensure easy access for all involved.

Once everything is signed and completed, the sense of relief is unlike any other. Instead of scrambling and worrying about legal issues in the last moments of a loved one's life, families can enjoy their final time spent together, knowing that everything has been taken care of, that there's a plan, and that their wishes will be respected. Getting the final bill isn't a stressful experience either: Cascade charges flat fees for wills rather than hourly rates, so there's no surprise when the invoice arrives. Estimated charges for various situations are clearly outlined on their website, as well as what's included with a will-based plan versus a trust-based plan.

The firm has a five-star rating on its Facebook page, and it's easy to see why. Whether they're working with a young married couple creating their will early, or someone at the end of their life putting a will together in short order, Cascade provides an experience that puts the client at ease so they don't have to worry about their future. The firm recognizes that the value they provide goes far beyond the estate plan they're creating and has designed the entire experience to be as frictionless as possible from beginning to end.

Cascade's investment in creating a better client journey helps ensure cases run more smoothly for everyone working at the firm as well. The lawyers and staff at the firm are committed to putting clients at ease at every stage of the client journey, and this helps them build a high level of trust that encourages clients to share key, sometimes deeply personal, details early on that could otherwise throw a wrench in things down the road. This is what it looks like to have deep empathy for your client at every stage of the client journey. Cascade has put serious thought into making the experience of creating a will as frictionless as possible, and it shows. If you were facing a difficult situation, would you prefer Cascade or the firm in the first example?

When a family is looking to quickly create a will during their loved one's last days, this is just one facet of what they're going through. They may also be dealing with funeral homes, hospitals, banks, and more. Their legal need is just one part of their experience. The client journey is a continuous experience from their point of view, and depending on the life event they're facing, there could be many more players at work besides your law firm. You fit into the client's journey, not the other way around.

Once you recognize this, you can uncover opportunities to improve the experience with your law firm and ensure you stand out as a provider.

The Client Journey

In order to best analyze the client journey, it's important to break it out in terms of stages that make sense to the client. The client journey is long and likely involves many more touchpoints than you'd expect. Again, the client experience is made up by *all* interactions a client has with your firm, whether directly with you or not. You might have an initial consult and meet with your client frequently throughout their journey, but they'll also read email updates, receive calendar invites, and get invoice follow-ups from your staff. This is all one continuous experience from your client's perspective, and one bad interaction can color their view of your firm negatively.

To avoid being overwhelmed, start slowly, and think through the entire client journey step-by-step. Really put yourself in your client's shoes. This will help you see the full extent of their journey and shines a light on potential areas that could be improved with a dose of client-centered thinking. At a high level, think about the beginning, middle, and end of the client journey. What does a client want at each stage?

At the start of the journey, a potential client is simply looking for a law firm to solve the legal issue they're having or to find out if they have a legal issue at all. They want to find a few options, feel confident that the lawyer(s) they're considering can actually help them with their issue, and anticipate that the experience working with them won't be difficult. They also need to be able to contact the firm easily and hear back on their issue in a timely manner.

In the middle of the journey, after a client has had an initial consultation and has signed on with your firm, they need clear communication and updates about what's going on with their case. Remember, your client doesn't know what they don't know about facing a legal matter. Depending on your area of practice, this may be their first time working with a lawyer, so they might be anxious about the experience.

At the end of the journey, they want to know what to do with the legal advice or legal deliverable you've provided. If it is a will, where should the client store it? How does it get executed? What does the client need to tell their loved ones? If they go through a divorce, how are the terms enforced? What should the client do if the terms aren't being followed? If they get a settlement in a personal injury case, when do they get their check?

If a firm doesn't explicitly provide this information, the client will be left confused and anxious—or annoyed—because they've paid for something but aren't aware of how to get the best use out of it.

Carefully designing each stage of the client journey with a client-centered mindset leads to an overall positive experience and more business for your firm. A mindset of empathy, first and foremost, followed by attentiveness, open communication, effortlessness, and partnership, helps cultivate the right client experience supported by internal processes at your firm that are as efficient and simple as possible for all involved. In order to start improving the client journey, think about where your firm is today. Here are some examples of what level of service would be provided by a client-centered law firm versus a non-client-centered law firm at various stages of the client journey. Which is your firm closest to?

Awareness: The Client Realizes They Have a Legal Issue
- At this stage, the client won't have any touchpoints with your firm.

Research: First Impression of Your Firm
- **Client-centered:** Marketing that clearly explains your services, your credentials, what's included, and an idea of cost. Easy to navigate website.
- **Not client-centered:** Overly salesy or nonexistent marketing. Hard to find contact info.

Consultation: Initial Meeting
- **Client-centered:** Thoughtful consultation, questions asked about client needs, rapport built, done on the client's terms.
- **Not client-centered:** Rushed consultation, few questions asked about client needs, done on the lawyer's terms.

Decision: Intake, Signing Engagement Letter, Expectation Setting
- **Client-centered:** Simplified intake that's convenient for the client. Easy to understand contract, e-signatures to

keep things simple. Expectations for payments, communications, etc., set with a clear welcome letter.

- **Not client-centered:** Tedious intake that requires paper forms and a visit to the office. Hard to read contract, no one to ask questions of, required to mail a signed contract or visit the office. No overview of what to expect.

During a Case: Communication
- **Client-centered:** Regular updates and easy to access information. Multiple communication methods that work for the client. Quickly answered questions.

- **Not client-centered:** Inconsistent updates. Limited communication methods. Long wait times for answers.

Billing and Payment: Clarity
- **Client-centered:** Clear, easy to understand bills. Multiple convenient payment options.

- **Not client-centered:** Unclear, jumbled bills. Restrictive, outdated payment options.

Review and Referral: Closing a Legal Matter, Asking for Feedback/Reviews
- **Client-centered:** Follow-up with additional information on what to do next. Asking for meaningful feedback on what could be improved or on what clients liked. Asking clients to leave a positive review if they had a good experience.

- **Not client-centered:** No follow-up. Blatantly asking clients to leave a positive rating without considering their experience.

Retention: Past Client Outreach

- **Client-centered:** Follow-up to assess current needs or changes to their situation.

- **Not client-centered:** Nonexistent.

If you find yourself identifying with more of the "not client-centered" examples, your clients likely aren't having a good experience, no matter the quality of the legal deliverable you're providing. You're also making things difficult for your staff and missing opportunities to work more efficiently. The flywheel is there, waiting to be turned.

Continuing the Client Lifecycle

Before I close off this chapter, I want to introduce one important concept to think about alongside the idea of the client journey: the client lifecycle. Throughout this chapter, we've talked about the client journey as something linear, something with a beginning and an end. But if you zoom out and think longer term, the client journey starts to look more like a circle than a line. The client journey could end when your client pays their final invoice (or when you ask for their feedback and a review of your services after that). Or you could stay in touch with your clients informally, stay abreast of their needs, and win their business again when they inevitably need more legal help.

The fifth value of a client-centered law firm—creating clients for life—comes into play here. It's absolutely worth putting in the effort to stay top of mind and proactively make yourself available for clients' legal needs so that you can continue the client lifecycle. If you've already gone through the effort of creating a positive client experience, and you've received plenty of positive reviews and referrals, it's a no-brainer to take this extra step.

Consider these two scenarios: A business retains a lawyer to guide it through a major transaction. All goes well, but when the transaction is concluded, the lawyer doesn't contact the business ever again: He simply thanks them for their business, wishes them well, and sends them on their way. It's not a *bad* way to end a client engagement, but it certainly doesn't leave the door open for further engagements.

Another business retains another lawyer, also to guide it through a major transaction. All goes well in this scenario as well, but this lawyer doesn't just leave it at that. He makes it clear that he's available for other work if needed and calls to check in yearly to see how the business is going, and if they have any further legal needs. It's a proactive approach, rather than a reactive one.

The former is a more transactional relationship, while in the latter scenario, the lawyer is a proactive partner. Which do you think business clients are more likely to remember and tell their friends about? Which lawyer do you think will identify more opportunities for legal work with their business clients? Which lawyer do you think is more likely to be rehired by their client, thus turning a client journey into a client lifecycle?

You do 80% of the work of practicing law and running a law firm up-front, while you're running a case, but the last 20% of the work—the low-lift, zero-risk act of following up and keeping in touch—is what could have the biggest impact on your bottom line. It matters to provide a good experience throughout the client journey, but a direct invitation for your clients to work with you again can make a big difference in how much your earlier efforts yield results.

As you're looking at the whole client journey, pay close attention to the end and how it might connect back to the beginning. With a bit of sustained effort to keep in touch and identify opportunities to tackle legal issues, your client journey becomes a client lifecycle, and your firm benefits even more from the positive experiences it creates. In the next chapter, we'll talk about a method you can use to create a detailed overview of the client journey to ensure you build an incredible client experience that makes your firm stand out from the competition.

" ———

You do 80% of the work of practicing law and running a law firm up-front, while you're running a case, but the last 20% of the work—the low-lift, zero-risk act of following up and keeping in touch—is what could have the biggest impact on your bottom line.

———   "

8

MAPPING THE CLIENT JOURNEY

TAKING A CLOSE look at the entire client journey can help you parse out which pieces of the client experience you can control and which you can't. With awareness of all the moving pieces, you can analyze your processes and improve them by looking for opportunities to provide a better experience.

What Makes a Map?

A client journey map is a visual representation of all the touchpoints a client has with your firm—directly or indirectly—on their journey from first thinking they might have a legal problem to retaining your services to finally closing the matter, paying their bill, and forming an opinion about whether or not to recommend you.

There are many different ways to structure a client journey map. It could be a line with plot points for various interactions and experiences, or a chart with different categories and

A bit of time spent thinking carefully about what your client goes through when they work with your firm can yield huge dividends—and is a key step toward becoming a more client-centered law firm.

plenty of detail for each stage of the journey. It could be a simple collection of touchpoints only, or it could include a complex range of elements like which department the client is working with at a given stage, questions clients might have, and pain points at each point or stage. The map could represent a linear journey, or a more convoluted one.

The exercise of client journey mapping helps many businesses, law firms included, to directly challenge their own assumptions about how clients experience their services. A client journey map brings awareness to issues, or potential issues, so that these interactions can be improved and businesses can provide a better experience to their clients. A good map puts everything out in the open, to make sure there are no blind spots. Often, the client's experience of their whole journey isn't entirely positive or negative—except in extreme circumstances. It's more likely that a law firm is doing well and providing a good experience in some areas but could use improvement in others.

Maybe a firm provides great service once a client is on board, but their intake process is cumbersome and outdated, making for a frustrating start. Maybe a firm is great at keeping clients informed by providing proactive, clear, and succinct email updates—but when billing time comes, it's not clear how clients can pay. What starts off as a great experience gets tainted by a poor billing experience at the end of the client journey.

Remember, one third of customers would stop giving their business to a company, even if they loved that brand, after *one* bad experience. As a law firm, this is critical to pay attention to—if a client isn't willing to give you repeat business, chances are they won't be referring other clients to you either. If one piece of the customer journey is off, your pipeline of new business is leaking. When it comes to your clients, ignorance is most definitely not bliss.

At the 2017 Clio Cloud Conference, Joshua Kubicki spoke about a law firm that had lost an insurance company client that had made up 40% of their business. Joshua was hired to help win the client back, and when he started to investigate what the problem was, he found that things were even worse: 57% of the firm's revenue was coming from insurance clients—and all of those clients were at risk.

When Joshua started digging into what the problem was, he found that even though the majority of the firm's work came from insurance clients, the firm's processes and marketing were that of a general services law firm. Staff and lawyers at the firm knew who their main type of client was, and what was bringing in business, but they hadn't optimized the experiences along the client journey to be geared toward that client. (Joshua also speaks about how the firm hadn't optimized its services to match the job its clients were trying to do. His talk is available for free on Clio's YouTube channel, and it's worth watching.)

So Joshua and the firm got to work redesigning many of the firm's internal processes, from how the firm captured and maintained information to how it billed clients—all to make the end-to-end client experience easier for *insurance* clients specifically. When they went back to the lost client, they also presented their solution in a way that clearly aligned with the needs of the person they needed to win over—the person in charge of procuring legal services—not the general, ineffable concept of an insurance company. The result? The law firm won their insurance client back, and later on, the client gave the firm an award for most innovative, value-added service of the year. In a sea of outside counsel, all more than capable lawyers, the firm Joshua worked with stood out—because they decided to pay close attention to the client journey and invest in creating a better client experience. A bit of time spent thinking carefully about what your client goes through when they work with your firm can yield huge dividends—and is a key step toward becoming a more client-centered law firm.

Stages of the Client Journey to Consider

The client experience is one long, continuous entity from the client's point of view. However, there are specific points along the journey where there's a natural shift in mental state, from when a client thinks they might have a legal problem to when they decide to hire a lawyer to when they choose a specific law firm, and so on.

Client journey maps often break the client experience out into different stages to make it easier to see how the client is feeling at various touchpoints with your firm, and to make the client experience more manageable to think about. For example, five commonly used stages are:

- **Awareness:** When a client first realizes they have an issue.

- **Consideration:** When a client is considering and comparing different solutions.

- **Decision:** When a client chooses and purchases a solution.

- **Retention:** When a potential client is now a paying client receiving a service.

- **Advocacy:** When a client is so pleased with a service that they recommend it to others.

The early stages are analogous to the buyer's journey, a framework for thinking about what clients think, feel, and experience as they move through the different stages of a purchasing decision. Businesses focus on analyzing and improving the experience at these stages with the goal of getting more clients to purchase their products or services, thereby growing revenues. Different industries use different stages, depending on what a typical client journey might look like. For example, a sample customer journey map from Rail Europe lists research, shopping, booking, pre-travel, travel, and post-travel as its journey stages.

When breaking out your client journey into stages, don't try to fit your clients' experiences into some preconceived norm. The five example stages above are great to use as a jumping-off point, but you'll want to consider more closely what a client is going through during each key interaction with *your* law firm.

How to Create a Client Journey Map

There are plenty of ways one can approach client journey mapping, but the main thing you'll need to do in order to make it a fruitful exercise is to establish an accurate picture of what the experience of working with your law firm is like for your clients.

It's easy to make assumptions about who your clients are, what they want, what they need, and what's most important to them, but as was made clear by the previous example, making assumptions about what your clients want from their legal experience—or worse, not really thinking about what they want at all—can lead to loss of business. If you're going to invest any amount of time creating a client journey map, you may as well make a map based on accurate data, or at least data that's as accurate as possible.

The goal is to cultivate a keen awareness of every part of your client's journey, and every multifaceted part of their experience at every stage: who else they're working with, what they feel, what they think, and what they believe they need. To start, you may also want to frame your mapping exercise to focus on one particular type of client or on one particular piece of the client journey (intake, billing, etc.) to make it more manageable. Once you get started, you'll almost certainly find that your clients interact with your firm much more often than you expected. Here are a few steps to guide you when creating a client journey map.

1. Involve a Cross-Functional Team

Chances are the lawyers at your firm aren't the only people who interact with clients. In fact, they may not even be the people at the firm who best know what your clients go through when they work with your firm, so make sure to involve people in a variety of roles. Paralegals, administrative assistants, receptionists, and even accountants will be able to share valuable information about how your clients interact with your firm. Part of the goal with customer journey mapping is to remove blind spots, and one of the best ways to do that is by comparing notes with others.

2. Think About Whose Journey You're Mapping

A central aspect of a client-centered approach is putting yourself in your client's shoes, but you can't put yourself in someone else's shoes if you don't know who they are.

First, inventory the types of clients you have. Do you usually handle no-fault divorces for amicable parents who want to get the paperwork over with and help navigating their new reality? Or do you usually represent divorcees in high-stress situations where there's a lot at stake? If you work with a business, think carefully about who your client is *within* the company. As with the insurance company example mentioned previously, the company is not your client; the firm Joshua worked with chose the people working in procurement as their "client," but you may think of your client as the GC or the CFO or the business owner, if it's a smaller company.

Then dig into who the person really is, insofar as it affects their experience with your firm. What are their wants and needs in the situation? Why have they chosen to come to a lawyer? How big of an expense is hiring a lawyer for them? What history, socioeconomic background, and life experiences are they bringing to the situation? Are there accessibility needs to consider? Rinse and repeat for as many different types of clients you can think of that you commonly deal with, grouped in whatever way makes sense to you. For example, if you work in business compliance focusing on small businesses, you might deal with a mix of restaurant owners, retail shop owners, and service providers.

As much as possible, don't assume you know the answers to these questions. Interview clients and staff to get an accurate picture of who your client is. The more you can collect this information firsthand, the more accurate your client journey mapping exercise will be.

3. Take an Inventory of Touchpoints

This is where the map gets interesting. Collecting information from as many sources as you can, brainstorm all the potential touchpoints (there are examples listed below to get you started) that make up the client experience with your firm from beginning to end. Remember to count points early on in the journey, when clients are just realizing they may have a legal problem, and points at the end of the journey, when they may be deciding whether to leave you a review.

Start at the beginning, and mentally walk through the entire client journey. In fact, it may be helpful to do this exercise in an environment outside of your firm. Walking a mile in your client's shoes can start with actually walking up to your office, attempting to experience every step in their state of mind.

In addition to your personal interactions with each client, you'll want to think of:

- Interactions with paralegals, administrative assistants, receptionists, and your accounting department
- Interactions with any tools your firm uses (e.g., client portals or e-signature software)
- Interactions with any services your firm uses (e.g., virtual receptionist services)
- Your website, online or offline ads, reviews, or directory listings that potential clients might see

This is where including a cross-functional team is helpful. Ask everyone for input, and you'll get a much more complete picture of the journey. It'd also be incredibly useful to go straight to the source and interview past clients to find touchpoints along the journey. You could use this as a starting point for your touchpoint mapping, or as a gut check to ensure your team hasn't missed any valuable touchpoints when brainstorming.

Once you've got a reasonably complete list of touchpoints, arrange them sequentially in the order of your client's journey.

	Doing	Feeling	Opportunity
Awareness			
Research			
Consultation			
Decision			
During a Case			
Billing and Payment			
Review and Referral			
Retention			

Example of a client journey map

4. Find out What Your Client's Experience Is at Each Touchpoint

Go through each touchpoint in the journey and interview some of your clients about their state of mind at each one. Were they feeling anxious? Frustrated? Worried? Relieved? Were they thinking that they didn't have enough information, or were they overwhelmed?

It's important, as much as possible, not to make assumptions. Your client journey map needs to reflect your *clients'* thoughts and feelings at each touchpoint along the client journey, not what *you* might think or assume is going on. That said, it's also important to look at how much of their experience is informed by pieces of their situation that you can't control and how much of it is informed by the quality of the service you provide. Clients may be coming to you with a lot of baggage, but well-designed touchpoints can make their experience better.

If a business owner receives a patent infringement notice, they're likely extremely anxious, worried about the future of their business, and questioning whether they have enough of a case. Your firm can't remove that experience—but a website that's difficult to navigate with little to no contact information and only a vague description of your services would make that experience worse—and would likely lead to the client looking for another firm to work with. A website that loads quickly, communicates services clearly, displays contact information prominently, and shows an appreciation for the experience the client is going through would make the potential client feel a little calmer and build trust with the firm.

The key is to build on the interactions clients have with your law firm to get a detailed, accurate picture of the entire client experience. From there, you can start pinpointing opportunities to improve the client experience and build a more client-centered firm.

5. Revisit and Revise

If you started with one type of client, remember to do this exercise with other client types as well. As your firm grows and changes, so will the client experiences you provide, so you'll need to consistently update your client journey map to ensure it's accurate, and to look for more opportunities to improve.

For example, maybe you've moved to online forms to make the paperwork portion of a divorce easier for your clients, because an early version of your client journey map showed you this was frustrating. You've done another map, and clients aren't frustrated with that process anymore—great!—but after that pain point is solved, something else becomes apparent: They're often worried, anxious, and showing symptoms of depression, which makes sense, as people often come to you for help with difficult separations. You put together a list of mental health resources and find a few good nearby counseling services to refer your clients to, including those for low-income clients. It didn't cost a thing but your time, and you've just increased the value you provide as a firm by zeroing in on what the client experience really looks like and thinking of a solution. This makes things easier for your firm as well: When clients are getting the support they need on all fronts, they're calmer and they more readily share key details that make it easier to get the settlement or the custody terms that they deserve. On top of that, they'll likely tell their friends about the lawyer that thought to provide support with mental health during a difficult time in their lives, and those friends will come to you if the need ever arises.

This is how you turn the flywheel: After you make one change, you uncover other opportunities to make more. You provide better experiences, get more positive reviews, strengthen your reputation, and get more business—and you keep finding ways to run your firm more efficiently so you can make even more improvements.

Creating an initial customer journey map is a good start, but it's the sustained effort in using this map to gain awareness of the end-to-end client experience, and in looking for ways to improve, that creates forward momentum to keep your firm growing.

A Client's Journey

To flesh out the example, let's look at a hypothetical client, Sarah. She's getting divorced, and there's a disagreement over property ownership. We'll follow her specific client journey through seven example stages, along with the touchpoints she has with the firm, what she expects, and what she's thinking and feeling at each stage.

1. Awareness

At this stage, Sarah and her spouse have decided to separate, but they disagree over what to do with the family home post-separation. Sarah wants to continue living in the family home with their children, but her spouse wants to sell the home and split the proceeds. He's asking Sarah to buy him out if she wants to stay in the home, but Sarah can't afford it. She's feeling anxious and upset: This is a serious problem, and she's not sure how she's going to handle it. She thinks she needs legal help.

She hasn't interacted with your law firm at this stage, but from her point of view, this is the start of the legal experience.

2. Research

Sarah starts looking for a lawyer. She's never been through a divorce, and neither have any of her friends, but she asks around anyway to see if they have friends who can recommend anyone. She's looking for *any* sort of reassurance that the lawyer she deals with will understand her and be able to help her. She's upset and apprehensive. She does some searching online and tries to contact some of the firms she finds. After some difficulty, she gets to yours.

This is Sarah's first impression of your firm: You have a website. It looks professional and it tells her what she needs to know. She searches for reviews and sees you have four out of five stars on Google. There's a recent reviewer who left a low rating, but most of the other reviewers mention how your firm was able to calm their worries and make them feel at ease—just what Sarah needs.

3. Consultation

Sarah heads back to your website to find your contact information. It isn't immediately visible, and she's frustrated for a moment, but after a bit of clicking and scrolling, she finds your phone number, email, and address, and calls in for an appointment. She books her appointment and receives an email with a link to an online form to fill out key information about her issue. It takes about 15 minutes to fill out, and she has to grab a few documents to get accurate information, but she believes it will be worth it.

She comes into your office the following week. The consultation is free, so Sarah doesn't worry about the cost, which is a relief. The lawyer she speaks to is kind. The consultation feels a bit rushed, and Sarah is slightly frustrated that she has to repeat some of the information she entered into the form and doesn't have the opportunity to explain her situation fully, but the lawyer confirms your firm can help her if she's interested, and Sarah cautiously trusts this lawyer. She didn't listen as much as Sarah would have liked, but she seems confident.

4. Decision

Sarah decides she'd like to hire your firm. She's a *bit* apprehensive about it, but she's extremely anxious about her issue and wants to get help as soon as possible. She fills out *another* intake form, covering some of the same information as the first one, and receives a letter of engagement to sign via e-signature a few days later. Sarah appreciates the convenience of an e-signature: It's how she signs most documents these days. She reads the letter carefully and calls the office to ask about a few things she doesn't understand before signing it. The letter also includes the terms of a payment plan for Sarah. The total cost of this representation will be more than what Sarah could afford in one shot, so she's relieved the firm offers the option to pay in installments.

She gets an email confirmation that her engagement letter has been signed—but no further information or follow-up from the firm. She doesn't hear anything for a few days and gets anxious, so she calls the firm. The administrative assistant she speaks to apologizes; she forgot to send the invitation for an initial meeting to share more details of her case, which has been booked for the following day. Sarah is frustrated because she'll need to take a day off work last minute. She starts to feel worried: Will this firm be on top of her case?

5. During a Case

As the case progresses, Sarah gets proactive updates on the case every so often, but not as often as she'd like, so she is often left wondering how things are moving along. After the initial consultation, Sarah's lawyer spends much more time listening, and Sarah feels at ease with her, but she knows her hourly rate is expensive, so Sarah is apprehensive about spending too much time with her. She's also feeling unsure and guilty about asking to keep the family home, but she can't afford to buy her spouse out. She believes she's doing what she has to do for her and her children and is getting support from her friends, but she could use some reassurance from a professional.

Finally, Sarah approves an agreement her lawyer negotiated with her spouse's lawyer. It isn't exactly what she wanted, and she doesn't quite understand why things were settled this way, but she's relieved to have come to a solution, and she's able to keep living in the family home.

6. Billing and Payment

Sarah receives her bill at the close of her case, and she's shocked. She knew the bill would be high, but it is much higher than she was expecting, and she doesn't understand half of the charges. Her anxiety spikes all over again. She frantically calls the office, asking them to explain what the charges mean, double-checking that scheduled meetings actually happened (after all, she almost missed her first meeting!). The call takes about half an hour, and at the end of it all, Sarah is feeling down but in agreement that the charges are accurate.

Sarah clarifies how much she'll owe the firm each month and asks if she can pay by credit card. The person on the phone says that no, the firm only takes payment by check, but that Sarah can mail it in so that she doesn't have to come by the office each month. Sarah rolls her eyes—she doesn't even know where her checkbook is. She's also confused: How does the firm have online forms and e-signatures, but they don't accept credit card payments?

7. Review and Referral

After her final payment, Sarah moves on with her life. She's the first one of her friends to get divorced, but a few years later, it starts happening more often. There are plenty of opportunities for her to recommend your firm, but she doesn't. If someone asks her outright about her experience with your firm, she shrugs her shoulders and says, "They were fine, I guess," and leaves it at that.

66

———

Analysis paralysis won't help your firm improve the client experience. Being a truly client-centered law firm is about taking action.

———

99

8. Retention

A few years later, Sarah has met someone new, and they're ready to move in together. But given her previous experience, Sarah wants to sign a cohabitation agreement first. Her new partner completely understands, and the two decide to hire a lawyer. Sarah thinks back to her experience with your law firm. She's not keen on the idea of searching for another lawyer, and she knows your firm does this sort of work. Sarah knows you'll get the job done, but she's reticent about the level of client service she'll receive. If she can get the same result elsewhere (for all intents and purposes) and have a better experience, why wouldn't she do that? Sarah asks a few friends if they have a lawyer they recommend, gets a few referrals, and ends up going with one of those options instead of reaching out to your firm again.

Putting the Client Experience Under a Microscope

Analyzing your client journey map will yield plenty of insights about the way your firm interacts with clients and how those interactions are perceived. Breaking the journey into stages helps to illustrate that the client's experience is made up of much more than their interactions with their lawyer. As you can see from the example, each stage can be broken down further to look at its smaller touchpoints. This further shows how the sum of minor interactions makes up the totality of the client experience.

In the example above, Sarah's experience wasn't *bad*. She got the help she needed, and certain aspects of her experience

	Doing	Feeling	Opportunity
Awareness	Dealing with the decision to separate from her spouse	Anxious and upset	N/A
Research	Looking for legal help	Apprehensive	Provide helpful information
Consultation	Contacting the law firm, filling out intake forms, having a consultation	Frustrated	Provide clarity, show empathy
Decision	Deciding to hire the law firm	Confused and ignored	Provide prompt follow-ups
During a Case	Interacting with the lawyer about her case	Unsure and guilty	Proactive communication
Billing and Payment	Reviewing her bill and figuring out how to pay	Shocked and frantic	Offer payment by credit card
Review and Referral	Considering whether to recommend the law firm to others	Unimpressed	Ask for feedback to improve
Retention	Deciding whether to work with your firm again	Hesitant	Follow up with the client

were even quite pleasant. But there were several key points where she wasn't getting the communication or convenience she needed, and that was enough to leave her with an overall lukewarm impression and a disinclination to recommend the firm in the future. At each stage of the client journey map for Sarah, there are opportunities to improve the experience for future clients.

One final note on client journey mapping: It's easy to get overwhelmed with *all* the touchpoints your firm may have, all the types of clients you serve, and all the different situations in which they might come to you. You could spend plenty of time overthinking where to start, what's most important, or how to structure a mapping project to account for all potential journeys. Don't do that. Analysis paralysis won't help your firm improve the client experience. Being a truly client-centered law firm is about taking action. After all, your clients see no benefit from the exercise of creating a client journey map—they only benefit once you start acting on insights from it.

With that in mind, it's absolutely fine to start small. Take an afternoon with some of your staff to get the skeleton of your client journey down, then iterate and update it from there. Or tackle the different stages of the client journey one by one. Or consider the different types of clients you serve and their journeys one by one. As long as you're taking *some* sort of action to gain as much awareness as possible of the experience your clients are going through, you're on the right track.

In future chapters, we'll talk about how to actually address issues you find within the client experience and come up with client-centered solutions, but for now, I'd like to discuss in more detail one of the most important aspects of running a client-centered law firm: empathy.

9

ON EMPATHY

IN CHAPTER 6, I talked about the five values of a client-centered law firm: developing deep client empathy, practicing attentiveness, generating ease with communication, demanding effortless experiences, and creating clients for life. These are all critical for running a successful law firm in an era where experience is king, but having empathy for your clients is far and away the most important. Client empathy is the force behind all that turns your law firm's flywheel of success.

When you have some empathy for your client, you get closer to understanding their situation, their pain, and their needs, and you're better positioned to look for solutions that make their experience a bit more effortless. When you focus intently on cultivating *deep* empathy for your client and their experience, you get an even clearer picture of what it is your clients *actually* desire and value from you, so that you can zero in on making their experience as great as possible without being distracted by things that don't matter.

It's crucial to pair empathy with action: If you don't communicate thoughtfully with them or take any action to improve their experience, then your empathy is of little help to your clients. Also, without action, empathy is of little help to you: If you're not taking action to improve the client experience based on your empathy for your clients, you're not creating an experience that drives clients to leave rave reviews and recommend your services to others.

Empathy and the Legal Profession

The word *empathy* is relatively new to the English language: It comes from the German word *Einfühlung*, derived from the ancient Greek word *empatheia*, meaning physical affection or passion. It was translated to English in 1908 by two psychologists from Cornell and the University of Cambridge, but it wasn't until the mid-20th century that empathy began to take on the meaning we know today—the capacity to put yourself in someone else's shoes and appreciate their feelings. Empathy is critical for helping us connect so that we can help each other through challenges, and it shows up often in the daily lives of skilled professionals such as lawyers.

In their book *The Future of the Professions*, Richard and Daniel Susskind talk about how empathy is so important that it's often one of the key objections to the idea that increasingly sophisticated technologies will negate the need for—or at least drastically change the work of—skilled professionals like lawyers, doctors, and accountants. Human empathy can't be replicated by a machine, and so there will always be a need for human professionals to provide face-to-face interaction, empathy, and support. I should note that, in the context of simply communicating that one feels empathy toward clients, Richard and Daniel argue that empathy is not a trump card that absolves the legal profession from having to change. They point out that not all professionals are truly empathetic (or even decent listeners), that empathetic support could easily be delivered by someone like a paralegal or legal assistant, that machines are more capable of providing the appearance of empathy than many would expect, and that many potential clients can't afford the services of a (maybe) empathetic service provider today. This is why it's important to not just develop client empathy but to *act* on it.

In our experience-driven world, client empathy is something that clients might not consciously pay much attention to when it's there—but it will be sorely missed when it's not. Showing sympathy by saying you're sorry to hear about your client's separation is table stakes, and that's certainly something a machine could do. Picking up on the fact that your divorce client has trouble getting out of bed and that their child has started to act out and delicately asking if they'd like a recommendation to a skilled family counsellor in their area shows true client empathy.

Empathy doesn't always manifest in direct communication. It might mean you paint your lobby a soft yellow because you've read that's a calming color and clients often come in stressed. It might mean you leave a selection of water and soft drinks out in the lobby because you're located in a warmer climate and clients are often hot and thirsty when they come in.

If you consistently cultivate deep client empathy and work to gain a clear understanding of the complexities of your clients' experiences, you can design incredibly painless experiences for your clients that help your firm stand out from the rest.

Empathy For the Whole Client Experience

Let's explore this concept with the example of a client who's buying a new home. They probably contact your law firm *after* they've decided to buy a home—what might they be feeling? Buying a home is an exciting milestone, but this client has also likely just made the biggest purchase of their entire life and may be riddled with doubt, anxiety, fear, and a ton of other emotions alongside all the excitement of owning a new property.

They've gone to open houses. They've seen multiple properties they liked and compromised on different factors to get an available property they could afford. Your client also went to a mortgage broker and got pre-approved for their first mortgage. They got progressively more anxious as the broker hastily explained a raft of rates and rules and options that they only half understood. Your client hopes they chose the right bank, but they're incredibly unsure.

Your client went back and forth with their spouse and real estate agent over how much to offer. They met in the middle, submitted their offer, and anxiously waited for a call from their agent. Finally, they got the call—their conditional offer was accepted, so they're almost homeowners! They then hurried to get a building inspector, who rescheduled three times before he was finally able to come to the house … but he finally made it. While the inspector found a few minor issues, all looks well, and the process moves ahead. It's at this point that they contact your law firm—they're really not up to searching for a lawyer after all they've been through, so they go with you because you're the firm their bank recommended.

Your client's experience of buying a home extends far after the close of their real estate transaction. Once they've closed on the sale of their home, they may do a final inspection before they take possession of the property, and then they'll pack up, move to their new home, and settle in their new neighborhood. On top of all that, if they have not sold their previous home yet, they'll have to go through the entire real estate transaction process again.

If you only think of the client journey as starting once you're hired, you'll have a very narrow view. You'll miss important context for how your client might be feeling, what they expect, and how they might react if you have negative news to share (e.g., if the seller failed to disclose that property taxes are not up-to-date for the house). You won't be able to truly empathize with your client, and you won't be operating as a client-centered law firm.

If those working at your hypothetical real estate law firm were to take the time to talk to past clients, ask about what their experience buying a home was like, and think in terms of the entire real estate purchasing process, rather than just the process of hiring a real estate lawyer, you'd have a chance to provide an effortless experience that would help your law firm stand out.

The actions you take as a result of having this empathy for your clients don't have to be complicated. Acting on empathy could be as simple as asking your client if they need a recommendation for a moving company, a storage facility, or a service to take away unwanted furniture or other items. If you were to keep a list of moving companies that you know and trust, you could easily make these introductions to clients and save them a lot of time and anxiety. You could also put together a short pamphlet with advice for a first home purchaser—involving the legal aspects of the transaction alongside advice on handling the emotional aspects of a housing purchase, knowing condo move in/out rules, and settling in once the purchase is closed and the client takes possession of the house. You could draft this document once and send it in an automated welcome email to new clients thereafter—it would mean next to zero ongoing effort from you, and an improved client experience for all new clients from that point on. At the end of each case, you could send another automated email to ask how the client's move went.

Creating this sort of experience is important for reviews and referrals, for more than one reason. When your clients see you in a positive light, they are inclined to recommend you, but the experience also simply needs to be good enough that clients remember you at all. With a bit of client-centered thinking, it's clear why this is the case: Instead of thinking of your client as simply that, your law firm's client, it's more helpful to think of yourself as a member of *your client's* team. Likely, your client is dealing with other businesses and professional service providers in addition to their lawyer. If it's a medical-related case, your client might be dealing with doctors, hospitals, and counselors in addition to your firm. If it's a personal injury case, your client could be working with an insurance company, their claims adjustor, and a physical therapist in addition to your firm. In the real estate example, your client is dealing with a mortgage broker, real estate agent, house inspector, and the bank.

Depending on your practice area, your client's emotions may be running high, and it may be difficult for them to remember each person they worked with a few years down the line. They also may not want to take the time to recommend every single person they've worked with—writing a detailed, positive review takes time and effort, and a client won't invest that effort if their experience was lukewarm. Essentially, you're competing with other service providers for referrals. If you can take a client-centered approach to the way you run your law firm, you'll be able to stand out from the other four or five service providers your client is working with as truly adding value—and as being worth recommending to others. When your real estate client's friend is buying their own home a few years later, your client might say, "I can't for the life of me remember the home inspector we used, but our lawyer was great. She helped with so much more than the transaction and really calmed my worries about buying a house. Let me give you her number."

Acting on client empathy isn't about going above and beyond for your client. In this example, I didn't suggest you pay for their moving company or show up personally to watch their kids while they packed. Instead, it's about zeroing in on what's most important to them during their experience, and focusing on making their journey more painless in a way that's efficient and cost effective for your law firm too.

Empathy in the Right Place at the Right Time

Think back to our example of Palace Law, the Tacoma, Washington, personal injury law firm that drastically reduced call volumes at its firm by providing updates via texts. This is a great example of what it means to engage in client empathy through communication.

Communicating clearly and often with your clients is a great start for creating a more client-centered experience: If a client is going through a serious and/or challenging life experience, keeping them in the loop on what's happening with their legal case can help them feel empowered and at ease.

But hammering your clients with constant communication doesn't mean you're being truly empathetic. Palace Law doesn't constantly inundate its clients with newsletters or marketing emails, or encourage staff to spend 15 minutes asking clients about their weekends each time they call for an update. They're sending a short text at the right time. Clients at Palace Law get a message notifying them that their check for their personal injury settlement is in, and in that moment, that's *all* Palace Law's clients want from the firm. The client knows that they've successfully filed their worker's compensation claim, or that their lawsuit has been successful, and they're just waiting for their check to close the loop. It's a thoughtfully designed experience based on empathy for what the client really wants. Palace Law delivers the right message to the client at the right moment—and it does so in a way that's efficient and cost effective for the firm as well as convenient for the client.

Locks Law Firm, a personal injury firm with locations in Pennsylvania, New Jersey, and New York, takes a similarly empathetic approach to client communications. The firm frequently takes on class action lawsuits, in which its clients can number in the thousands. Previously, when a client would call in to speak about their case and then immediately call back with a follow-up question, it was difficult to direct their call to the right person with 50-plus lawyers and staff working on a case and all calls going through the front desk. Directing calls was time consuming until the firm began using Clio's Firm Feed, a live stream of activities performed on different matters for different clients by everyone at the firm, to quickly figure out who each client was trying to reach. Using the Firm Feed, Locks' receptionist can quickly identify who a caller was speaking to (based on recently logged activity in Clio) and then direct their call to the right person—saving headaches for both the firm and their clients.

The concept of following empathy up with action in the right place at the right time is powerful, because anyone at a law firm can do it. If you're an associate at a larger firm working mainly in bankruptcy, you could draft a short guide on dealing with the emotional aspects of bankruptcy, have it sent automatically in a welcome email to new clients, and ensure you share statistics on how common bankruptcy is in your area, so that clients don't feel quite so alone. If you're a receptionist or administrative assistant at an immigration firm, and you notice that clients often make mistakes and get frustrated on paper intake forms, you could transfer the questions from that sheet to a Google form in an hour or two and let clients fill in their information on an iPad or from the comfort of their own homes (and save yourself a lot of time deciphering chicken scratch and typing in information from paper forms). Or if you're a personal injury attorney, you could set up automated texts from your business number to alert clients when their checks come in.

Once other lawyers and staff at your firm see the increase in personal positive reviews and referrals you'll inevitably have from offering more client-centered experiences, they'll follow suit, making your entire firm more efficient, profitable,

*You work incredibly hard
for your client, but if they don't
see that work as part of their
client journey, they're not getting
a full picture of the value you're
providing. Perception matters.*

and successful. The journey toward a rapidly spinning fly-wheel of success starts with just one push. Cultivate empathy for your clients, watch for opportunities, and act in the right place at the right time, and you'll create a successful, more client-centered practice.

Communication Best Practices

Of all the ways you can act on empathy to create a good client experience, good communication is one of the most important. This goes well beyond client meetings. You're likely communicating with your clients in more ways and more often than you might expect—in newsletters, on your website, and even through the wording you choose at the top of intake forms. Empathetic communications will be different at every law firm. For a family law firm, it might mean taking the time to express sympathy for clients going through difficult divorces and communicating in a way that is mindful of their emotional trauma. For a business firm that does "run the company" work for long-term clients, empathetic communication might mean keeping meetings as short as possible. That said, there are a few key principles to follow to create a positive client experience through empathetic communication.

Communicate Clearly

Your clients aren't lawyers. They don't know the law like you do, and they might not have much experience with the legal system at all—that's why they've hired you. It's important to empathize with this, and to act on this reality by providing simple communication. With thoughtful, clear discussion about their case, your clients will feel empowered and at ease knowing that they understand what's in play with their legal issue. Plain language is not just for legal writing: It's also something to be mindful of when writing emails, letters, forms, and even invoices.

Even if your clients *are* comfortable with denser, more complex concepts (say, for example, you're a lawyer who represents lawyers or an outside counsel who regularly works with GCs), they'll still appreciate clear and succinct communication. No one likes wading through a lengthy email full of meandering sentences, industry jargon, huge blocks of text, and disorganized ideas. Keep sentences short and sweet, only include one or two ideas per sentence, and use common words instead of four-syllable ones. Highlight crucial details your client needs to understand, and be clear what you're providing for added context.

And there are benefits for your firm too: Succinct communication means your clients will "get it" right away and have fewer questions about bills, emails, contracts, and agreements, so less time will be spent on follow-up.

Be Mindful of Perception

If you provide a free 15-minute check-in with a client but don't include it on their invoice, in your client's mind, did it ever really happen? You work incredibly hard for your client, but if they don't see that work as part of their client journey, they're not getting a full picture of the value you're providing. Perception matters.

This isn't a call to boast about all the hard work you've done, to pressure your clients into expressing gratitude for your expertise, or to bombard them with marketing messages. It's a call to be mindful of how your clients perceive your services and to clearly, objectively communicate the work you're doing so that they know they're in good hands.

For example, Katy Young of Ad Astra Law Group, a San Francisco–based law firm focused mainly on business litigation, thinks of invoices as an important communication tool to show clients the value of her service and consequently cut down on follow-ups and requests for discounts. One of Katy's key values is to always show her clients what they're paying for—and what they're not. Katy indicates where she's changed her hourly rate, added a discount, or provided a service for free. She also includes just enough detail for the client to know which conversation, email, or meeting they're being billed for. That way, if a client gets sticker shock, they can easily see what they're paying for and have a ready explanation for why their bill was higher than expected.

Many of Katy's clients are footing the bill in their business litigation suit themselves: They're self-employed, so they may not be eligible for legal aid, even if their business is bankrupt. Handing over tens of thousands of dollars for a legal bill that only vaguely outlines services would cause anyone's anxiety to spike, but for a small business owner in this situation, that feels even worse. Katy uses her bills to demonstrate her empathy: She's thought through the client experience and has tailored this communication touchpoint to make things a little easier.

As a bonus, this also makes internal processes easier for Katy's firm: With clear bills—that include "freebie" phone calls, emails, and the like—there are very few clients who call to question or dispute charges, cutting down on administrative work for her staff. Draw attention to the value you provide to clients, rather than expecting them to read your mind or pick up on hints, and you'll help them feel like they're getting the most out of their spend on legal services.

Remember the Importance of First Impressions

Finally, remember that you only get one chance to make a first impression.

When a potential client is looking for a lawyer, their emotions are often running high. The last thing they want to do is to wade through confusing bar directories or websites and contact a handful of lawyers, only to never hear back from any of them and have to start the process over again. And yet, this is the experience many clients face: unclear websites, difficult to find contact information, little to no pricing information (unless they're in a jurisdiction that requires that pricing information be displayed), and, to top it all off, an extremely delayed follow-up on their request—or no follow-up at all. According to research conducted for the *2019 Legal Trends Report*, 60% of email inquiries sent to law firms asking for help received no response at all, and of those that did respond, 71% were unsatisfactory in terms of the information provided. Of law firms that received phone calls as part of the study, only 56% picked up, and of the 39% of calls that went to voicemail, a whopping 57% didn't call back within 72 hours.

Respond promptly, and put extra thought into your firm's first contact with a client, and you'll communicate that you empathize with their situation, which helps put them a bit more at ease. In turn, this will also help your law firm stand out from the competition. No matter where or when your client is first contacting you, make sure that you're clear about what you do, how you usually help clients, and how to contact you. Consider providing pricing information too: For most people, legal services aren't affordable, so having an idea of what the expense will be ahead of time helps.

More importantly, talk about what you do in terms of what your clients need, not in terms of your expertise. Your client doesn't want to hire a real estate lawyer: They want to settle into their new home as soon as possible and rest easy knowing that there are no issues with their title to the property. If you can show that you empathize with their situation and that you're willing to discover what they need right from your first interaction, you're building trust and creating a frictionless experience from the get-go.

Knowing What Your Clients Want

Your clients expect a cohesive, effortless legal experience in addition to sound legal advice and/or a satisfactory legal deliverable. Giving them that experience means thinking intently about their full client journey, and using that tool to build and implement empathetic processes.

This is where Jobs to be Done theory, introduced in Chapter 4, can be helpful. Instead of thinking about what your clients want as a concrete *thing*, think about their wants as *jobs to be done*—what they hope for in the outcome of their situation from their perspective, rather than from the perspective of the sorts of services you offer. Figuring out what job your client is trying to get done is an exercise in true empathy. In order to get it right, you really need to put yourself in your client's shoes. Talk to your clients. Think from their perspective. Ask past clients questions about their experience, if they're willing to give you time. Many people have trouble articulating this, but it's possible to determine something yourself based on whatever insights you *can* get from your client. We'll cover this idea more in-depth in upcoming chapters.

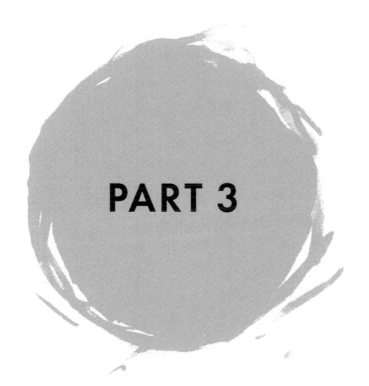

PART 3

10

DESIGNING YOUR CLIENT-CENTERED LAW FIRM

IN PART 2, we talked about what makes a law firm client-centered: the five values of being client-centered, the tool of journey mapping to better understand the client experience, and, above all, the importance of empathy. Those concepts alone provide a valuable foundation for the mindset shift that needs to happen in many law firms, but they won't tell you what you need to *do*—how to actually become a more client-centered law firm.

In Part 3, my goal is to give you a framework to adapt and innovate at your law firm. We start with a set of steps to improve the design of your client experience. In the next chapter, we'll talk about how to manage (and encourage) the cultural shift to a client-centered law firm, and after that, we'll talk about how to measure your success, learn from and improve upon changes you've implemented, and continue turning the flywheel.

Becoming a client-centered law firm *does* require a mind-set shift. You'll notice that many of the steps here encourage embracing ambiguity rather than rushing ahead to solutions. ("Embrace ambiguity" is one of the core values of the renowned international design firm IDEO.) You don't need to know the answer right away; in fact, being open to not knowing will get you to a better solution in the end. What I'm proposing here, I realize, will be a major shift for some firms where processes have always been well defined and slow to change. If your firm has been operating one way for a long time, it will be challenging to take a new direction. It's all in the way you think about things. Lawyers have keen analytical minds, an intricate knowledge of the law, and a strong sense of how to apply the law in different situations. But approaches taught in law school aren't the best approach for every area of business. If you can accept that you won't have all the answers right away, and that building a client-centered law firm will be an ongoing process, you'll be better positioned to adapt and stand out from your peers. With a few proven tools from the business world to help you make the right changes at your firm, you could design a law firm and a legal experience that sets you and your firm apart.

Design Thinking and Jobs to Be Done

Design thinking and Jobs to be Done theory are extremely helpful frameworks for solving business problems and innovating in meaningful ways.

Jobs to be Done is about figuring out what "job" your clients are truly trying to hire you for. We covered this in

Chapter 4 with the milkshake example: McDonald's marketing executives thought customers were hiring a milkshake for the "job" of providing a tasty treat, but they were actually hiring milkshakes for the job of giving them something to do on their long drive to work—and the job of keeping them full until lunch.

Design thinking is, essentially, about getting clear about which problem you're trying to solve, exploring multiple solutions, and acting on that. Design thinking prioritizes action: It's better to prototype a solution, get it in front of clients, test it, learn from it, and create an even better solution than it is to labor away in a silo hoping to get it perfectly right the first time. According to Stanford's d.school, there are five stages of the design thinking process—empathize, define, ideate, prototype, and test—and designers are meant to iterate and move forward and backward in the process as needed.

If you'd like to dig deeper than the overview given here, a number of leading legal thinkers have created resources that apply design thinking and Jobs to be Done theory to issues within the legal industry: Margaret Hagan, a lawyer, designer, and director of the Legal Design Lab at Stanford University, is a strong advocate for a design-driven approach to legal innovation. Her online book, *Law by Design*, provides an excellent introduction to design concepts and design processes for lawyers. Cat Moon, director of innovation design for the Program in Law and Innovation (PoLI) at Vanderbilt Law School, teaches legal problem solving through the lens of human-centered design thinking and is passionate about using design to make the practice of law better. She has curated a wealth of helpful articles and resources at legalproblemsolving.org. Michele DeStefano, a professor of law at the University of

Miami, is another major proponent of design thinking in the legal industry: She founded LawWithoutWalls, which facilitates workshops for lawyers, business professionals, and students to create innovative solutions to real business-of-law challenges, and her book *Legal Upheaval* provides an excellent guide to creativity, collaboration, and design thinking. Joshua Kubicki has spoken extensively about Jobs to be Done theory and how it can be applied to improve the way law firms are run and the experiences they provide. Many of his interviews and presentations can be found online.

Jumping straight from one well-defined system of management to another will only bring a set of new, albeit different, challenges to be addressed. Conversely, leaving old systems behind and jumping into the great unknown with *no* plan isn't a recipe for success either. Without a framework to grapple with all the possibilities and ambiguities before you, you'll either fall into old habits—solving problems the way you always have and ending up at oddly similar solutions—or you'll rush to pick a direction and a mindset out of necessity, which might not lead to the best new model for your firm. What's an innovative law firm to do? Following frameworks that are well defined but that encourage innovative thinking will provide a "just right" amount of guidance to help innovate in an experience-driven world.

Design thinking and Jobs to be Done theory both prioritize understanding the problem at hand. Jobs to be Done theory demands a lot of research to get there: You can't just ask your clients what they want (although talking to your clients will be a valuable part of your research). Observe them in action as well, taking stock of when, where, and how they use your legal services. With design thinking, the first step is *defining* what problem to solve—and doing the research needed to be confident that you're solving the *right* problem. For example, your legal clients may say that they want to meet with you more often, but if you looked into why they wanted to meet with you, you might find that the information they're looking for could be easily conveyed through more frequent email communications, or that they're looking for peace of mind that could be provided through regularly scheduled meetings rather than as-needed ones, so that your client would know when to expect an update from you.

That said, design thinking and Jobs to be Done theory also both stress the importance of not jumping to conclusions when trying to find a solution for the identified problem. They start with getting a very clear view of the problem to be solved, or the job to be done, but this doesn't mean knowing the solution ahead of time—finding this takes testing and iteration.

Neither design thinking nor Jobs to be Done theory condones the practice of *implementing* solutions without knowing what problem you're trying to solve or why you think a new process or tool will work for your organization. When thinking about improving the client experience, it's easy to be swayed by the idea that new tech tools will make things run smoothly, or that a fancier office will make your clients feel more at ease, or that a certain bill format will be easier to read for your clients.

But if you don't stop, observe, and get to the heart of an issue, you could be wasting your time and money trying to solve the wrong problem—or worse, no problem at all. It might seem easier to charge ahead with solutions so that you can get to results faster. Certain issues might seem obvious. But haste makes waste. If you don't take the client-centered approach of talking to your clients and doing the research up-front to ensure you're solving the right problems, you'll find yourself two steps back rather than one step ahead.

The best way to avoid this is to stay grounded in the values of a client-centered law firm: Start by creating a client journey map, and then identify specific touchpoints that could be better designed so that they'd lead to an overall better client experience. Then make sure that your approach is informed by design thinking and Jobs to be Done theory so that you stay true to the first and most important value of a client-centered law firm: developing deep client empathy. If you do that, you'll turn your firm's flywheel of success with every change you make. Over time, you'll build the type of client-centered law firm that has a significant, sustained advantage over competitors.

Steps to Designing for a Better Client Experience

If I could only provide one tip for designing for better client experiences, it would be this: start. If you're at a larger firm with a forward-thinking mindset and you can afford to embark on an in-depth client journey mapping exercise for multiple situations and an action plan for multiple touchpoints that need improving, that's wonderful. If you have an afternoon to sit with a group of staff and roughly map out the client journey, with the intention of picking one issue along the journey to zero in on, validate, and try to improve, that's excellent too.

But either way, you absolutely do not need to wait for everything you might think you need in place. Even if you are embarking on an in-depth exercise, you can start with a minimum viable customer journey map that you can use right away, rather than toiling away stage by stage and waiting months before you have anything you can act on. Get started, start with what you can, and iterate from there.

Even one change informed by frameworks like design thinking and Jobs to be Done theory can make a powerful difference for your clients and your staff—if your clients are a little happier, you get a few more referrals than normal, and your revenues are a bit higher than normal following one or two small changes to the way your firm operates, you can bet that those who were apprehensive of change will be much more willing to jump on board after that.

Any effort to meaningfully improve the client experience starts with tackling *one* problem: one touchpoint, one stage of the journey, one way that your firm engages with its clients.

1. Review Your Customer Journey Map

Before you can start to improve any one piece of the client experience, you'll need some level of context for the rest of the client journey. This might be a full-fledged client journey map, as we discussed in Chapter 8, complete with your firm's touchpoints with clients along different stages of the journey and insights into what your client experiences at each stage. Or it might be something less intricate: a quick and dirty map made up of insights, reflections, and brainstorming from a two-hour afternoon session with your staff. Either way, having a visualization of the big picture will help you prioritize an issue to work on that matters to both your firm and your clients, rather than a hypothetical issue plucked out of thin air.

Take a look at all the touchpoints, ideally with a group of people working in various functions. Which client experiences stand out to you? What surprises you? What feels a little gritty to look at? What touchpoints make you think, "Wow, *that's* how we do things?" These are strong indicators that you've found a touchpoint to be improved.

Reviewing your client journey map for potential issues might feel like a tough look in the mirror. It's important not to use this as an opportunity to blame or shame anyone responsible for creating a certain process. If you're reviewing the journey map in a group session with people in various roles within the firm (which I recommend you do, if possible), set the tone of the conversation at the start: If all staff feel comfortable raising ideas and issues, you'll get better results.

If you find a lot of issues with the client experience at your firm, don't feel discouraged—simply being open to the idea of running a more client-centered law firm and taking the first steps toward improving the client experience sets you apart from your peers.

Whether you choose to tackle a single situation, a single stage of the client journey, or a single type of client with a specific type of case your firm sees often, make your choice based on where an improvement could have a meaningful impact on the full client experience, meaning a better legal experience for your clients, a more efficient and pleasant work environment for staff, and a positive impact on your firm's bottom line. Once you've chosen your focus, it's time to start digging in.

2. Gather Information

How often do you talk to your clients about whether they're getting what they need from your law firm? If the answer to that question is "rarely," then it's time to correct that. Ask your clients what they're missing, whether or not they liked specific parts of working with your law firm, and if they have anything else they'd like to share. Beyond listening attentively, you also have to look—read between the lines, observe differences between what your clients say and what they do, and watch for body language that indicates that there are more jobs to be done that your clients haven't been able to articulate.

It takes research to figure out what your clients want, but this is an investment that will yield dramatic returns for your law firm in years to come. And you don't have to do it all at once: You can start small, and you'll be surprised at the valuable insights you'll find.

You'll also be surprised at how willing your clients are to give you their time. When Clio was still in beta, my business partner Rian and I asked lawyers to request access and attend an onboarding interview where we could learn about their practice. We also asked them to let us take them through a demo of Clio.

These demos were meant to last 30 minutes, but often they extended far beyond that. Lawyers would spend one, two, or even three hours giving us real-time feedback on the product. I was blown away: They could be billing hundreds of dollars per hour for their time, but here they were giving us feedback that would improve their experience.

If that's what some of your peers are willing to do to improve the experience they have with their office software, just think of what your clients would be willing to share in order to improve the incredibly stressful experience of facing a legal matter for themselves, their friends, and their family. And once you have that feedback to act on, you'll be much closer to designing a more client-centered experience at your law firm.

Spending hours on the phone getting feedback from your clients on how your law firm works, day in and day out, may not be feasible, and that's okay. There are smaller ways to gather feedback. Send out a short survey. Select 10 past clients and offer to take them out for coffee or a meal so that you can pick their brain. Make it easy for staff and associates to share impromptu feedback they get from clients. Pretend you're a client and see for yourself what the process is like, or ask a client to let you watch them use a client-facing tool so you can see it in action. The bottom line: ask. Any insight is helpful insight, as long as you consider the source, stay curious, and avoid jumping to conclusions about the problem being faced.

Asking Good Questions

Getting good insight from clients requires asking good questions—questions that reveal the true nature of your clients' experience.

Ask Open-Ended Questions
(Who, What, When, Where, Why)

This might seem like a given, but it's deceptively easy to slip into asking yes/no or leading questions. Remember you're gathering information, not narrowing in on what a potential problem might be. Keep your clients talking with open-ended questions. Ask who they were with and who they talked to for advice before hiring you. Ask what they were doing. Ask

66 ____

"Is there anything you'd like to add? Anything we didn't cover here that you'd like to chat about? Is there anything else?" Sometimes, a client won't have anything else to say, but other times, this question can be a goldmine.

____ 99

where they were when they first heard about you and what their initial impression was. Ask where they most often are when you contact them with updates, and how this impacts their daily lives. It's the simple questions that yield surprising answers and point you in the direction of unforeseen solutions.

Ask "Why" Five Times

Asking "why?" again and again isn't just for your four-year-old niece: Asking "why" multiple times is extremely valuable for getting to the heart of the issue at hand.

The Five Whys interview technique was created by Sakichi Toyoda of the Toyota Motor Corporation as a method for finding the root cause of a given problem. It's part of the Toyota Production System, a set of Toyota's management philosophies and practices developed with the goal of reducing waste in manufacturing. Many of the principles underlying the production system have gained popularity far beyond the auto manufacturer, with University of Michigan professor Jeffrey Liker publishing a book on the principles in 2004, called *The Toyota Way*.

The idea behind the Five Whys is this: The answer to the first "why" might lead to something that looks like it explains the problem, but in most cases, if you look a little closer, it's another symptom. Asking why again leads to another deeper cause, and then another, and another, until the questioner finally reaches the root cause of the problem.

For example, if you ask a divorce client why they never make it to your meetings on time, they might apologize and say they just keep losing track of time. At first blush, it might look like the solution to this problem is for your client to try a little harder to stick to their schedule, but you can dig a bit deeper. When you ask why they keep losing track of time, they might say that they've been feeling down and having trouble concentrating lately, and when you ask why they've been feeling that way, you might discover that your client has been struggling with mild depression and would prefer to talk over the phone or meet over video where possible, to save themselves a trip to the office. Only when you know the root cause of the problem can you start to effectively look for solutions.

Ask The Same Question Twice

"Why" isn't the only question you may want to ask more than once when trying to get insight into the client experience. If your client gives an overly vague answer to a question, or if their body language tells you they're holding something back, don't be afraid to casually ask the same question again in 10 to 15 minutes. Often, the first ask gets your interviewee thinking, while the second or third ask prompts them to spit out the answer that's since been percolating in the back of their mind.

All that said, don't pressure your clients: Their job isn't to define the problem *for* you. Their feedback gives you insight into their experience so that you can define these things yourself.

Ask If There's Anything Else

This question comes in all shapes and sizes. "Is there anything you'd like to add? Anything we didn't cover here that you'd like to chat about? Is there anything else?" Sometimes, a client won't have anything else to say, but other times, this question can be a goldmine.

No matter how thorough your client journey map and your client interviews are, your client will always have thoughts, feelings, and priorities that you can't possibly know about.

Maybe you've got a long-running case, and your client moved, but something fell through the cracks when they changed their address and they've had to coordinate with the people at their previous residence to get their mail. Maybe your client has a friend whose lawyer texts them updates, and they wish you did that too. Ask if there's anything else before the interview ends, and you'll find those nuggets.

Best of all, this is perhaps the most empathetic question you can ask your client, because it's a truly open-ended way of asking for their perspective.

3. Define The Problem

In order to come up with the most effective solution to any issue with the client experience, you have to be clear about what problem you're trying to solve. Gathering information from your clients helps you to validate that the issue you're looking at actually exists and to clarify what the problem is.

Once you've conducted all your customer interviews, spoken to staff, and otherwise gathered information about the piece of the client journey you're focusing on, look for takeaways that will help you clarify the problem. *Why* are your clients frustrated at this point in their journey? Are there patterns in what different clients and staff are saying? What are they really getting at with their feedback? Are there personal values, circumstances, or jobs to be done that could help you get to better solutions?

The goal in this step is to use your insights to create a clear definition of the issue you're trying to solve.

In design thinking, this is called a problem statement. With Jobs to be Done theory, this is framed as a job to be done rather than a problem. Either (or both) may work for you and your firm depending on the nature of the thing you're trying to address. For example, if steps 1 and 2 of this process reveal that your immigration law clients feel frustrated because they don't know what's going on during their case, a problem statement might be "My green card application was submitted, but I haven't heard anything from my attorney in weeks and I'm starting to feel incredibly anxious," while a job to be done might be "Help put me at ease throughout the process of applying for my green card."

Problem statements and jobs to be done can be written in first person, second person, or third person, as long as the focus is on the *client* and their perspective. I tend to write these types of statements as if the client was speaking, because that makes it feel like the client is in the room—a powerful way to keep you and any teams focused on the client experience (as opposed to a slow swivel to not-so-client-centered focus on what "we" offer).

Statements also need to be specific enough to be actionable but broad enough to allow for multiple solutions. "I'm frustrated with my experience at this law firm" isn't a good problem statement because it's too broad, but "I only like to communicate via email and I really wish my lawyer responded to my emails right away" doesn't work either because it only leaves room for a few specific solutions.

Your problem statement and/or the job to be done will focus your team and provide a meaningful framework for the rest of this exercise. If there's any stage you want to be careful not to rush, it's this one: Take your time to review the information you've gathered and craft a problem statement. Your efforts to improve the client experience will yield much better results.

4. Brainstorm Solutions

Once you've settled on a problem statement, it's time to come up with a few solutions. In fact, it's time to come up with a *lot* of solutions. Design thinking prioritizes coming up with as many solutions as possible right off the bat and narrowing down options later. This approach is valuable because it encourages teams to go beyond the obvious and come up with unexpected ideas to meet client needs. Your problem statement, or your job to be done, will keep the conversation from getting so broad as to be unmanageable.

This stage of building a client-centered process is a great opportunity to have a bit of fun with your team: Giving a jolt to their creative brains and making sure everyone feels comfortable sharing out-there ideas will get you the best results.

Get poster boards, and let everyone draw huge mind maps related to the problem statement. Write ideas on colorful post-it notes and paste them around the room. Divide everyone into teams and have a competition to see who can come up with the most ideas. Set a timer and get everyone to write down their own ideas as fast as they can, and then open up the floor for discussion to see what else surfaces. If your team is spread across different locations, you may also want to use collaborative brainstorming apps like Popplet or WiseMapping.

Encourage everyone to get all of their thoughts out in the open, without judgment. Then start sorting through the suggestions and pick one (or a few) to move forward with. Ideally, one person should make the final decision about which ideas move forward, to avoid analysis paralysis, but ideas that aren't used initially can be explored further at a later time.

There are a few ways to make this choice: You can pick the solutions that logically best match the problem statement, or the solutions that are most innovative, or the solutions that seem most cost effective, but whatever your methodology, make sure the proposed solutions align with the values of a client-centered law firm. Develop deep client empathy, practice attentiveness, and demand an effortless experience for your clients.

5. Design a Process Prototype

This is where the actual design piece of design thinking comes in. Now that you've decided on how to solve your problem, you need a way to make it a reality.

Designing a prototype might sound difficult, but there's no need for it to be overwhelming. For the purposes of improving the client experience at law firms, your solution will probably be a *process* prototype (you'll likely be designing a process, rather than an object or a computer application).

Unless you're starting a brand-new law firm, you're likely redesigning a process rather than creating something from scratch. Whether intentionally designed or not, the process your law firm already uses is the one your clients are used to, and unless it's absolutely terrible, making incremental adjustments to that process will be a better approach than throwing it out the window.

For example, if your immigration clients want more regular updates on their case, and they're used to communicating via email, start by setting regular reminders for associates to send update emails, even if it's to confirm that there are no updates. Don't default to launching a new app that requires clients to sign in so that they can check for updates and read them there. With this big of a switch, it would be near

"   ⸻

*No matter how perfect
a solution appears,
and no matter how deeply
you believe it will lay the
groundwork for a better client
experience, there's almost
always an unexpected result
that you won't discover until
you put it into action.*

⸻   **"**

impossible to assess which improvements were helpful to the client experience and which were harmful.

I'd also recommend against building your own technology to solve for a client journey touchpoint, unless your firm has the resources to invest in building a quality proprietary app or software platform (and even then, I'd be hesitant). Client communication, e-discovery, accounting, credit card payments, overall practice management, even AI-driven legal research: There are plenty of secure, quality tools available built specifically to handle the day-to-day needs of lawyers. My point is, do your research before you hand over thousands to a developer or startup accelerator, because the solution you seek could be readily available with existing products.

Remember what you're designing is just a prototype. The goal is to build something quickly, learn from it, and iteratively improve this touchpoint rather than getting to the perfect solution the first time around. Take a client-centered approach here: Your client is at the core of your law firm, and your law firm provides a valuable, protective layer around the core, so *both* need to be taken care of. Your prototype needs to work for your client, and it also needs to be cost effective and efficient for your law firm—considering both factors will lead to a better overall solution.

To that end, think about how you'll test the success of your process prototype *before* you test it. What will success look like? If you can't answer this question right away, that's okay, but make sure you have a plan to measure success before you roll your solution out to your clients.

6. Test

So, you've made a client journey map. You've analyzed it for gaps and opportunities for improvement. You've done client research, come up with a problem statement, brainstormed, and crafted a beautiful process prototype that you *know* is going to make things better for your firm and clients. But there's one more step you'll need to take before you roll your solution out to clients: You have to test it.

No matter how perfect a solution appears, and no matter how deeply you believe it will lay the groundwork for a better client experience, there's almost always an unexpected result that you won't discover until you put it into action. Testing is part of the learning process, and it helps you design a better solution—if your prototype doesn't work, go back to step 5 and build a new prototype. Don't rush forward with a solution that has serious issues, e.g., a solution that makes things easier for one set of staff but needlessly creates extra work for others, or a solution that updates clients on their case but makes it unclear what, if anything, they need to do next.

When testing, it's worth keeping in mind that proving true causation or correlation between changes to firm processes and how clients feel will be difficult for most law firms—or at least more resource intensive than is useful. Ideally, you'll have a defined metric and a goal for improvement, but if you don't have one, that's okay. Looking for critical errors in the system is a good start, and you can continue engaging with clients to see whether their experience improves over time.

To test your new process prototype, try it yourself! Depending on the size of your firm, have staff do it too. Aside from illuminating potential issues with your new process, putting yourself in your clients' shoes can provide some incredibly valuable perspective. Even better, if you've got a few clients that you have strong relationships with, or a helpful close friend or family member, ask them whether they'd be willing to test out your new process. This is the best way to test your process, since, even if you try to put yourself in your clients' shoes, you may still make assumptions that lead you to gloss over issues. Listen to feedback, and implement fixes that ensure the new process runs smoothly.

Most importantly, remain objective. Don't succumb to confirmation bias when looking at test results. There's a tendency to favor information that confirms your existing beliefs, and if it's a solution you feel strongly about, or an idea you came up with, it can be easier than you think to fit the results to that solution—but that won't give you the best outcomes.

Once you're confident that your process improvement is ready to be seen by the rest of your clients, move on to step 7.

7. Implement

At this point, the third value of a client-centered law firm—generate ease through communication—is the most important. And if you have empathy for your clients, it's easy to see why.

No matter what state the client experience you provide is in right now, your existing clients are used to it. Any change will require some adjustment for both your clients and your staff, so introducing your new process with an intentional communication plan will be critical to its success.

Notify existing (and recurring) clients *well before* the change happens. Make sure they're aware of what's changing and how they can get the most out of it (especially if it's a change that requires action for them to see value, like introducing the ability for them to check for new details on their case whenever they like).

With new clients, implementing change is a little easier, because they won't have preconceived notions about how things run at your firm. Rolling out your new process to new clients also provides you with a valuable opportunity: Without preconceptions, new clients will have an entirely different experience, so you can see how your new process works with different cohorts of clients. For example, existing clients might not like a new process because they're simply used to something different, but the same process might be received very differently by new clients. You can see the difference by tracking various customer sentiment metrics, which we'll discuss in Chapter 12.

The key thing with both new clients and existing ones is to ensure that staff are set up to run the new process smoothly. Have a plan to notify everyone within your law firm of the change and to communicate how this change will affect their day-to-day. This is especially important for firms that are large enough that not everyone is involved in designing the process improvement at hand: If all staff and associates don't know that change is coming, they can't be prepared to implement it successfully for clients.

A few unexpected issues may pop up that didn't during the testing stage, and that's okay. Know that things won't be perfect the first time, and be prepared to make a few tweaks when the process rolls out to clients, so you won't be caught on the back foot. Building a client-centered law firm is an ongoing process. As long as you're willing to take on a mindset that lets you continually adapt and improve, you're on the right track.

8. Repeat and Iterate

At the beginning of this chapter, I briefly mentioned the five stages of a design thinking process, which are more general than the steps that specifically apply to law firms outlined here. One key characteristic of those stages is that they're not meant to be linear. Designers can move forward and backward throughout the process as necessary, and you can do this too.

For example, testing may teach you more about your clients and help you develop deeper empathy, leading you back to the information-gathering stage of the process. It may spark more creative ideas, leading you back to the brainstorming process. It may illustrate a subtle misunderstanding of the job your clients are trying to get done, leading you back to redefine the problem.

The process isn't rigid and linear, because the world isn't rigid and linear, and neither are your clients' experiences. Improving a given touchpoint along the client journey isn't a one-off endeavor. It's an ongoing process where the client experience improves slowly but surely over time. And as the flywheel turns faster—your firm gets more revenue as a result of happier clients giving positive reviews and attracting more new clients to you—you'll have more resources to create an even better client experience.

Once you've kicked off this process for one touchpoint along the client journey, repeat the steps as needed to address other gaps. Maybe you've improved your communications during a case, but your billing still needs work. Or maybe your clients love your website and find it easy to sign up with you but would much prefer if you offered immigration services for a flat fee. Each new process you tackle will require a bit of up-front effort, but it gets easier once the flywheel is moving and you start to iterate on the work you've already done. Once you get in the habit of consistently making improvements to design for a better client experience, you'll only be creating a more and more client-centered law firm and reaping compounding benefits.

Start Somewhere

If you're reading the steps here and feeling a bit apprehensive about how to put them into action at your firm, I hear you. Lawyers and legal professionals work long, stressful hours, and part of what allows things to keep moving forward is a dependable process. For busy legal professionals, even the most minute changes in workflow can put a strain on your workday. But if old, outdated processes are slowing you down, making you less competitive, and creating frustrating experiences for your clients, avoiding the need to change is avoiding the inevitable.

The important thing is to get started. While it's definitely ideal to follow the steps above, anything is better than nothing. If you've only got an afternoon to look at the client journey, choose a problem, and brainstorm possible solutions, that's perfectly fine. Just be sure to carefully define the problem so that you come up with a process improvement that keeps it simple as well.

Maybe you change the font size of your letters to make them easier for your elder law clients to read. Maybe you add an intake form to the homepage of your website so potential clients can contact you more easily. Maybe you update your voicemail message with an email address where clients can

Change is hard, and it's even harder when you really, REALLY don't want to do it. Just as it's important to develop deep client empathy, it's important to have empathy for others at your firm who are scared of, intimidated by, or just straight-up resistant to change.

reach you to get a faster response to their query—or maybe you try sending updates via text message so that your clients don't have to call in the first place.

In the words of Edmund Burke, "Nobody made a greater mistake than he who did nothing because he could do only a little." Little things, over time, make a difference. The key is to treat the five values of a client-centered law firm as your guide. Start developing empathy and making changes when and where you can, and demand effortless experiences for your clients. For a time, the change will be imperceptible. But one day, you'll walk into the office and notice that your clients are happier, your staff are happier, and your receptionist is busily fielding calls from more clients than you've had for quite some time.

That said, getting used to continuous change requires a big shift in mindset—one that might be difficult if you've always had specific rules and processes to follow. In the next chapter, we'll talk about how to manage the shift to a more client-centered law firm—whether you're a partner leading the charge or an associate who sees the writing on the wall and wants to bring their firm into the 21st century.

11

SHIFTING TO A CLIENT-CENTERED CULTURE

AFTER OVER 10 years of working in the legal industry, I can safely say that the rumors are true: Most lawyers do not like change. I can't tell you how many stories I've heard of lawyers outright refusing to accept a new process, a new tool, or a new mindset without even considering the potential benefits to be had. There are many reasons for this, of course. Lawyers are famously risk averse, and being risk averse often translates to being change averse. But unfortunately, this deeply ingrained resistance to change could hold entire firms back—even if it only comes from a few staff or lawyers.

The *real* challenge of building a client-centered mindset is getting buy-in, or at the very least some openness to the idea, from everyone at the firm. You can craft the most client-centered processes in the world, but if those who are meant to use them won't adopt them, they can't make an impact.

Depending on how receptive your firm is to innovation, getting buy-in might be an uphill climb whether you're a firm of 10, 100, or 1,000 people. But there's a tremendous opportunity in pushing for this change. If you're reading this book, and you want to be an innovative legal thinker, you're still in the minority in your industry: Become a legal change-maker now, and you can be part of the push that gives your firm a competitive edge by putting it at the forefront of the client-centered revolution.

After reading this chapter, you'll have a solid set of tools to help you drive change, no matter how slowly you need to go and no matter how steep the hill you need to climb.

The Five Values of a Client-Centered Law Firm, Reapplied

The five values of a client-centered law firm are useful in more ways than one. They'll keep you focused on your clients, so that you continue to grow and thrive as a truly client-centered law firm, but you can also look at the five values of a client-centered law firm to guide you in approaching people *within* your firm.

Think back to Chapter 5, where we talked about how Zappos and Starbucks have made humble commodities much more valuable by packaging them as part of incredible, effortless client experiences. Their successes haven't been the result of a client-first-at-all-costs focus: Both companies have also invested heavily in creating a good *employee* experience and in ensuring that everyone who works there values the client experience. There's no reason your law firm can't take this same approach.

Change is hard, and it's even harder when you really, *really* don't want to do it. Just as it's important to develop deep client empathy, it's important to have empathy for others at your firm who are scared of, intimidated by, or just straight-up resistant to change. That might feel difficult when you're in the middle of an argument, or when a partner is still refusing to log into your firm's new tool three months after implementation. But patience, persistence, and communicating what's in it for them will break down egos and create openness to change.

Here's how to use the five values of a client-centered law firm to guide you to buy-in for new client-centered processes from everyone at your firm.

Develop Deep Empathy

Much like a client journey map helps you understand the day-to-day challenges of your clients, it's important to understand the day-to-day challenges of staff and lawyers.

People won't refuse change because they want to see what you're doing fail. They'll resist change because they feel misunderstood and unheard. If you don't understand them, why should they try to understand a shift to a client-centered law firm? Maybe administrative assistants don't have the patience to learn new processes because they've tried new ways of working in the past with mixed results. Maybe paralegals don't want to participate in client journey mapping and brainstorming sessions because they feel their ideas won't be valued. Maybe that partner who simply refuses to adopt any new technology is terrified because he had a friend who lost critical client data because he wasn't performing backups of his on-premise servers and was nearly disbarred as a result.

Before kicking off a serious client-centered endeavor, talk to your partners and colleagues to learn what their challenges are. Ask them to take you through a day in their life, and ask questions to fill in the gaps. Make an effort to develop deep empathy for others in your law firm, and you'll build trust, create stronger relationships, and leave people open to adopting more client-centered processes.

Practice Attentiveness

When learning about the day-to-day experiences of staff and lawyers at your firm, don't take everything at face value, and don't immediately brush off concerns as backward-thinking. Listening only works if you do it well, and others in the firm will only trust you and buy in to your projects if they feel heard. Ask plenty of questions. Watch for body language and other cues that indicate there might be something they're not sharing. Some people may feel more comfortable sharing feedback privately; an anonymous survey might yield more results than 1:1 interviews—you know your firm best, so keep your culture in mind when deciding how to collect feedback.

If someone has a lot of direct feedback to share, remember that, depending on your firm's culture, this may be the first chance they've had to share their thoughts on how things work. It may take some digging to get past initial complaints and reach the heart of the issue. As hard as it may be in the moment, the more patient and empathetic you can be, the more successful you'll be.

It's important to be open to the needs of those within your firm. When their needs are met, they'll be set up to perform better and provide excellent client experiences—but if they feel unheard, and if they feel like their experience at work is getting worse at the expense of a better client experience, you'll have a hard time making any changes stick.

Finally, keep an open mind. You may have ideas about what needs to change, but you may hear different responses about what important day-to-day challenges are for everyone at the firm. If you hold on to your own assumptions about what's wrong, you might miss key opportunities to improve both the client experience and the working lives of staff and lawyers at the firm. Stay open and objective, and you could unlock a goldmine of opportunities.

Generate Ease With Communication

Your colleagues are incredibly smart, dedicated people who work tirelessly to run legal practices and uphold the law in our society—but "mind reader" isn't on their list of skills. No one will know what you're planning, when it will be rolled out, and what's expected from them—unless you communicate those things.

This is where empathy comes in handy. Put yourself in your colleagues' shoes, and ask yourself what you'd want and need to know about a new tool or a process change. How early would you want to know about it? *What* do you want to know about it? Are status updates helpful or distracting? Then validate these assumptions by actually asking!

Also, remember that your colleagues don't have the same background knowledge as you. You may have to explain what a client journey map is before undertaking a brainstorming session, or explain terms like CRM, lead, and conversion rate if you're implementing a new client intake system. Assume your colleague has zero knowledge of the concept, term, process, or tech you're talking about, and explain it in plain language. It's much easier to speed up a discussion if you discover everyone already understands what you mean than it is to regain your audience's attention after going too quickly and being faced with blank stares.

Demand Effortless Experiences

Just as you'd demand effortless experiences for your clients, a successful client-centered law firm demands experiences that don't cause excess stress for the people who work there. This might require a bit of creativity beyond the obvious answer to problems, but that's what the steps in Chapter 10 are for. If clients want more regular updates, you could ask staff to get on the phone 20 times per day—but if you dig a bit deeper to see that what clients really want is more access to information and your staff really want to spend time on more impactful work, you can solve the problem by providing access through a client portal. If you're looking to keep better track of client contact information, and ensure phone numbers and addresses are always up-to-date, you could ask assistants to painstakingly update the info across various systems and documents—or you could use a system that allows you to update info in one place and see the change everywhere.

You'll only create a truly client-centered law firm if you empower everyone at your firm to provide great experiences. The new tech tool you're implementing might help your colleagues do their work twice as fast, but if they're not sure how to set it up or use it, or if they don't see the value in it, they'll quickly go back to their old way of doing things, so provide training and clearly communicate what's most important.

Create Advocates for Life

The first time we introduced this value, we talked about creating clients for life. But you can also apply this to lawyers and law firm staff. The double meaning here is intentional: You want to help lawyers (advocates) grow and create a positive work environment so that they stay with you, instead of leaving after a few years, and you also want them to advocate for your firm as a great place to work.

A critical piece of any business's ability to attract top talent is its hiring brand. Law firms need to create good client experiences so that past and existing clients refer new clients to them, but it's also worth creating good experiences for your staff and/or colleagues so they refer other smart legal professionals to you. It's about having empathy for what others on your team need out of their working lives.

Note: this does *not* mean you need to adopt the approach of Silicon Valley tech companies and add a ton of extraneous perks to pamper employees. It means respecting the value of how they contribute to your firm, creating opportunities for growth, and building a positive environment by making your firm's clients as happy and pleasant to work with as possible. If you can help automate and streamline the more repetitive pieces of the job, you'll allow everyone to spend more time on what they really want to be doing—and you'll create processes that are more cost effective for the firm to boot.

Keep the five values of a client-centered law firm in mind as they apply to your clients *and* your colleagues and staff,

> *A client-centered law firm can't be built in a vacuum, and it definitely can't be built alone.*

and you'll be much better positioned to implement impactful change that sticks at your firm.

Getting Others Involved

Sparking change at your law firm, designing more client-centered processes to create better client experiences, *and* orchestrating the shift in a way that's empathetic toward colleagues who are apprehensive of change? That's a tall order. But it's more doable than you'd think: Whether you're a new associate sharing this book to sow seeds for acceptance of client-centered thinking or you're the managing partner investing in a full-scale project and trying to inspire staff to get on board, every effort will make a long-term difference for your firm and the legal industry. But it's easier if you don't do it by yourself. A client-centered law firm can't be built in a vacuum, and it definitely can't be built alone. When you build trust and work together as a group, there's less resistance to moving forward.

Heidi Gardner, a former McKinsey consultant and Harvard Business School professor, now a distinguished fellow at Harvard Law School, speaks about the importance of building trust and breaking down silos at law firms in her book *Smart Collaboration*. Teams are more effective than individuals at solving issues and getting things done. Heidi provides hard evidence that law firms that collaborate are more profitable and successful; her research shows that as more practice groups serve a single client, that client generates exponentially more revenue for the firm—not in the context of cross-selling but in the context of working together.

The way that you get others on board could start with a weekly meeting to discuss new ideas in the legal industry. It could be a task force focused on a discrete project to improve one process to be more client-centered, with the intention of proving out the concept to get more buy-in later. If you run a smaller firm of 10 people or less, get everyone involved in defining new client-centered values specific to your firm (more on that in the next section).

If you're a solo lawyer with no staff, you won't have the issue of getting buy-in from others within your firm, but it will still be useful to collaborate with others about how to build a more client-centered firm. Reach out to friends from law school or trusted colleagues. Go to bar association events and meet other lawyers in your area. Even talking to a few trusted friends or family members who are not lawyers can be helpful—especially if they've had experiences as a client in your practice area.

The more you can collaborate with others to bring about client-centered change at your law firm, the better you'll set yourself up to succeed.

Redefining Who You Are

Having a clear set of values is something that's contributed in a big way to Clio's success. Up until about five years through Clio's journey, our values evolved organically and were implicit. Everyone at Clio was roughly on the same page, and it didn't feel necessary to write them down. But at a certain point, there were a lot more new faces at Clio, and having our values agreed upon by the team and formally written out seemed like a valuable reference point to guide us. I don't think we would have retained our culture as Clio has scaled without that touchpoint.

On the face of it, defining your law firm's values might seem like a fluffy, pointless exercise. But that couldn't be further from the truth. In fact, it can be one of the hardest exercises because of the unique perspectives and strong opinions your team will bring to it. Whether you've thought about it at length or not, you already *have* a set of beliefs and values, and so does everyone else working at your firm. If you haven't talked about them and come to a consensus about why the firm exists and what it should focus on, you risk divergence and conflict as people make more and more varying assumptions about what should guide key decisions at your practice.

It's only when the *reasons* for becoming more client-centered align on a deep level with the values of everyone at your firm that you'll get the commitment needed to successfully shift to a more client-centered practice—and one that can improve your bottom line.

The five values of a client-centered law firm are a great starting point for firms generally, but getting everyone aligned on values that are specific to *your* firm will be much more powerful. Whether being client-centered primarily means you'll improve access to legal services, or whether it means you'll become a streamlined, competitive, powerhouse law firm set apart by the experience you provide, getting clear on why it makes sense for your firm to be more client-centered will help you reach your goal.

Get people involved: Talk to everyone at your firm if you work with 10 or fewer people, and a representative from each practice area and job function if you're at a larger firm.

Make sure everyone is heard, and that potential blind spots are uncovered, by either talking to people individually or scheduling a group conversation where it's made clear that everyone's voice is valuable. Ask why they do what they do, why they believe the firm exists, and what they believe their purpose is at work.

Capture everyone's ideas in a brainstorming session, in a shared document, or in a document you create yourself to translate what you hear into potential values, but in the end, distill it all down into three to six values described by one short sentence each. (You can add bullets below to elaborate, but at a high level, each value needs to be easy to remember.) Likely, this limit will force you to cut a few ideas—which is why this is a valuable exercise in determining what's most important to your firm.

Defining your firm's values isn't a mission-critical step in becoming more client-centered, but if you have the time, resources, and willingness to do it, it will be a big help toward ensuring everyone gets on board and *stays* on board with new client-centered processes.

Making Change Stick

Once you've put in all the effort of rallying team members toward client-centered change, reviewing the client journey at your firm, and creating client-centered processes, you'll want those processes to be put into practice. You'll also want lawyers and staff to continue using those processes for a long time, and to speak up about any improvements needed. But the gap between a process change and successful implementation can broaden to a wide chasm if not handled well.

As business strategist Heather Gray-Grant has put it, "Many projects lose the respect and confidence of a firm not as a result of the decision, but as a result of poor implementation. Don't let your change project suffer this fate after working so hard to get to this point."

When planning how to implement a new client-intake process, a new billing format, or a new tool to help clients schedule meetings more easily, keep the five values of a client-centered law firm top of mind. It's all about having empathy toward those at your firm whom new changes will affect and showing that empathy through clear and effective communication.

This doesn't mean simply providing information to other staff and lawyers and hoping for the best: The time, the place, and the way change gets communicated all matter. At the end of the day, your staff and/or colleagues are learning something new that might drastically change their day-to-day. The tips below might read like common sense, but unfortunately, I've seen that it's all too easy to let these pieces of the implementation process fall by the wayside under the stress of a heavy caseload, the pressure of end-of-month billing, or one of a myriad other pressures law firms face.

Communicate Change Early

Surprises can be fun but not when they impact how you do your day-to-day work. It might be tempting to try to push a new process as soon as possible, especially if you believe it's going to have a significant, positive impact on your firm, but you'll have better results if you let everyone warm up to the idea first.

Even if you don't have all the information right away, communicate that change is coming as soon as it's approved and a plan for implementation is being put into motion. Share it in an email, or bring it up at a team meeting—whatever works best for your team. Then provide updates and reminders as you get more information and get closer to the date, and ensure a training session is scheduled prior to the official switch.

This warm-up period also gives you a chance to bring around those who are skeptical of the new process. If you meet a lot of resistance, don't get discouraged. Listen to concerns. Answer questions thoughtfully. Think carefully about what's in it for these individuals, not just the firm, and communicate that. The more you can do to influence how everyone feels about change before it starts, the more likely it is that your implementation will succeed.

Put Your People at the Center

You might be introducing the new process that kicks off the client-centered revolution at your firm, starts spinning the flywheel, and brings your firm long-term success, but you're not at the center of your new process implementation—the people *learning* about the new process are. Just like you're shifting to be client-centered, you can help make sure change sticks by putting your staff and colleagues at the center when educating on a client-centered shift.

The overall success of the firm is important, but at the end of the day, people are motivated by what directly affects them. Frame any communications in terms of why adopting new processes will make your colleagues' day-to-day lives better. What's in it for them? Depending on whether they're an administrative assistant, an associate, a partner, or someone else, this might mean a more pleasant workday,

66 ———

The overall success of
the firm is important,
but at the end of the day,
people are motivated by what
directly affects them.
Frame any communications
in terms of why adopting
new processes will make your
colleagues' day-to-day
lives better.

——— 99

less of a monotonous task they don't enjoy, happier clients on the other end of the phone, or simply less overhead and a healthier bottom line for the law firm they own. Pinpoint what motivates your team, and frame any conversations and training sessions in a way that highlights this.

Make Important Information Stick

Lawyers need to know the details of the law, but in work and life more generally, people don't remember every little detail. Whether you're sending an email communicating a small change to the reception area that people might notice, or whether you're planning training sessions on how the firm will use a cloud-based tool to collaborate across multiple offices, the message will only stick if you highlight what's most important.

A good starting point is to have a clear answer to the following question, before you send anything, say anything, or plan any sessions: What's the *one* thing you want everyone to take away from this? Write the answer down, and use it to guide the way you communicate your changes going forward. You can pick two or three secondary items if the change is more complex, but make sure it's still clear that your number one item is most important. If you share too much information without stressing the key message, you risk distracting team members with nice-to-have but inconsequential information, at the cost of them missing the crucial piece.

When deciding the one key takeaway, think about what your colleagues *need* to know to be successful—and, if applicable, what could be a risk for your firm if someone were to get it wrong. For example, if your firm is going to start using an online scheduling tool to allow new clients to book their own free consultations, make sure everyone knows that it's important to keep their calendars up-to-date so that no one gets double booked.

Another important factor in making new information stick is in the way you organize the new processes you share. As you may or may not have learned from your school days, you can only remember so much at any given time. That's because new information initially gets processed by your working memory before it is transferred to your long-term memory—and while your long-term memory can hold a potentially unlimited amount of information for an unlimited period of time, your working memory can only process a small number of information units, and this information is forgotten in less than a minute. However, you can "hack" this limitation by organizing information into chunks.

You can put this trick to work by presenting your new client-centered change in a way that makes sense. Maybe your new billing process involves a lot of minor steps, but these can be grouped into a few higher-level ones, making the whole thing easy to remember. Maybe you're switching from 15-minute free consultations to flat-fee consultations that are more flexible on time, because you've found clients would prefer to pay a small fee and know what they're getting into before they hire you. As a result, you anticipate many questions staff may have to handle that they haven't faced before, and you want to prepare them with answers, but these types of questions and your suggested responses could be grouped into distinct categories to make everything easy to recall.

You'll only be able to capture a limited amount of everyone's attention to communicate new client-centered processes and how to be successful. The more thoughtfully you craft your communications and training sessions to highlight what's important, the more success you'll have.

Make Training Interactive

You want the relevant people at your law firm to be able to do new tasks, work with new tools, and follow the new procedures your client-centered changes demand. Practice increases both confidence and competence. Accordingly, if the new process or tool you're introducing is more complex, work an interactive aspect into your training program. Allow your team members to follow along with what you're doing on their own computers, and then find time to allow them to practice on their own before the new program rolls out to clients. Role-play certain situations with half the group pretending to be clients that the other half is working with.

Watching your team practice can also expose gaps in understanding. There's nothing worse than designing a brand-new process and crafting a careful training plan only to have key aspects of the process be lost in translation, so that it falls apart when it's put into action. Give your team a chance to get some hands-on experience with your new client-centered changes before they go live to the world, and you'll mitigate this risk.

Advocate for Ongoing Support

Communication and training for new processes shouldn't be a one-off exercise. Once your new website, client welcome package, or feedback collection program launches, it will be easy for your team to slip into old habits if they don't feel supported, or if they don't see the impact of their efforts.

Once your new program is out in the wild, staff and colleagues will encounter situations you didn't account for. Whether they use the principles underlying what they've learned in their training with you to inform a new approach to the situation or they revert to how they did things in their previous process depends largely on how much ongoing support is provided. For example, if your receptionist is confused by your new online client intake system, or by the iPads clients use to fill out forms, are they likely to help a confused client troubleshoot the issue, or will they shake their head, hand over one of the paper forms they've stashed in their desk, and manually enter the client's data later in the day, like they used to do? To put it another way, you can't just give your colleagues a fish: You've got to teach them how to fish, so that they make choices that continue to turn the flywheel of success.

There are a few ways you can approach this, depending on your role within your firm. You can provide ongoing practice sessions to get colleagues to use client-centered principles in unexpected situations, or you can advocate for time to be made for these programs. You can also make yourself available as a resource, holding "office hours" for those who might have questions. Finally, you can create champions by enlisting those who've bought in to your client-centered change to provide encouragement and answer questions from those who are still hesitant, so that you're not going it alone in the endeavor to make running a more client-centered law firm stick.

Whatever you do, don't stop pushing for client-centered change at your law firm. Even if you can only do a little at a time, you'll keep up momentum and keep pushing the flywheel, so that your firm will reap the benefits of a more experience-driven approach.

A Lasting Commitment to Change

In this chapter, I've talked a lot about how to enact a client-centered shift through the implementation of more client-centered processes—like the ones we talked about designing in the last chapter. If you're in a position to use these chapters as a playbook to successfully start the shift toward becoming a more client-centered law firm, that's wonderful. But having that level of authority within your organization is not a prerequisite to kicking off your client-centered journey.

You can absolutely ignite the client-centered revolution at your law firm in much smaller ways. You can provide better client service to the extent that you're able in your own role, and share your positive results with others. You can look for opportunities to gain feedback from clients and share that feedback with your team. You can share statistics from this book, like the fact that one third of customers would leave a brand they loved after just one bad experience, and get the okay for the team to spend an hour every other week sharing client feedback and brainstorming ideas to improve the client experience.

What's needed will be different for every law firm, and you'll see different challenges depending on how open to innovation your firm is currently. If you're in a traditional firm where people still track their time on paper, or use spreadsheets, you'll have a lot of mind-changing to do up-front. But if you strongly believe your firm needs a client-centered approach to thrive in the experience-driven era, it simply makes sense to push onward—whenever, and however, you can. Once your efforts are in motion, you can start measuring success, showing results, and making stronger arguments for why the client-centered way is the way forward.

12

MEASURING SUCCESS

ONCE YOU'VE WORKED hard to implement client-centered changes to the way your firm runs, how will you know your efforts have been successful? Tracking and measuring the effectiveness of your efforts might seem like a nice-to-have or just one more thing to add to your plate, but measuring your success is one of the most important things you can do to be, well, successful. As Peter Drucker said, what gets measured gets managed.

It's easy to make assumptions about how well you're doing. As evidenced by some of the statistics mentioned earlier in this book, lawyers have been doing it for years when it comes to how they communicate with clients, what their clients value, and how satisfied they are with their lawyers. It's also easy to psych yourself out when you're actually doing well: It might be frustrating to hear about clients calling in with a lot of questions about a new client-facing tool, but in the long run, as staff work out the kinks of the process, the questions dwindle, and things run more smoothly than ever.

Having a way to measure the success of your client-centered initiatives will keep you objective about what's working and what isn't, so that you can build increasingly client-centered experiences without getting sidetracked.

There are multiple ways to measure your success. Both qualitative and quantitative feedback are important, as they inform each other. It's also helpful to look at both lagging and leading indicators of success. And it's important to have perspective on the limits of your ability to definitively measure causation or correlation for any one initiative within your firm.

That said, you don't need to become an expert in statistical analysis. Any effort to objectively measure the success of your client-centered efforts will provide valuable insight to your firm and will set you up for success as the flywheel continues to turn.

Getting Feedback

One of the best ways to get a view into how well your client-centered processes are doing is to simply ask for feedback. In order to know whether any new process or tool is effective, you need to know that it's working well for both your clients *and* the people working at your law firm.

Feedback from Your Clients

The hours-long sessions Rian and I had taking feedback from clients while building Clio were invaluable to the early success of the product, and even today, we prioritize having conversations with clients and collecting their feedback as much as possible. The only way we can build the best product possible is by getting as much insight as possible into what our

66 ———

You don't need to become an

expert in statistical analysis.

Any effort to objectively

measure the success of your

client-centered efforts will

provide valuable insight to your

firm and will set you up

for success as the flywheel

continues to turn.

——— 99

clients need, and getting their direct feedback is one of the most valuable ways to do that. This approach simply makes sense for any business, including law firms.

Ask your clients how they felt about your service. How easy was it for them to get their legal matter resolved? What did they like or dislike about the new tool your firm has rolled out? What did they think of your new website? Anywhere you feel there's a gap in your understanding of the client experience, or where you feel you're making assumptions rather than looking at what clients have to say, start by asking a question. Also, be open to clients who reach out with unprompted feedback for you. You might think of a ton of questions to ask your clients, but you won't be able to think of everything, and being open to unsolicited feedback can help illuminate unlikely blind spots.

For example, I once went on a trip to Greece where my family and I stayed at the Hilton in Athens. My wife and I were traveling with our young children, and we were meant to have two adjoining rooms—one for them, one for us. However, when we checked in late at night after a long flight, we found that our rooms were actually across and down the hall from one another. On the face of it, this might not seem like *that* big of a deal. But it was—we didn't want our six-year-old daughter wandering the halls of a hotel in Greece trying to remember which room we were in if she had a bad dream in the middle of the night. I'd made a very specific request to have adjoining rooms when I made the reservation, so I decided to speak up about it. It took about half an hour of back-and-forth with the manager, but we were upgraded to the presidential suite at the hotel! There were no adjoining rooms available, so this was the only option for solving our problem.

What could have been a very frustrating experience turned out to be an incredible one, but only because I was willing to have an uncomfortable conversation. Not everyone is willing to do so. How many other families had a similar experience, and instead of giving their feedback directly to the Hilton staff, left a negative review or vowed to never stay at a Hilton again? The hotel clearly thought it was acceptable to separate our rooms without letting us know beforehand, so they either hadn't gotten feedback before that this wasn't okay or hadn't gotten feedback often enough to see it as a real issue.

If one client gives feedback that the format of your bills is hard to read, or they can't find your contact information on your website, they're likely not the only person having that issue. In fact, according to Lee Resources International, for every customer who complains, there are 26 more who've remained silent. Client feedback is a gift, because it exposes areas that could be affecting the client experience negatively for many people and losing you positive reviews and referrals.

Is there an opportunity to improve the client experience with a process change that wouldn't mean much extra work for your firm and might actually make things more efficient for you? It's listening and looking for these golden nuggets of feedback that could set your firm apart from the rest.

Feedback from Staff and Colleagues

While it's best to get feedback directly from clients wherever possible, it can also be extremely valuable to collect feedback from staff. You can send out surveys, book one-on-one meetings with client-facing staff, hold group focus sessions, or chat with others in the breakroom about what they see clients experiencing. A wide sample from various roles is best. Do what you can, depending on the time, resources, and authority you have within the firm.

How easy was it for them to complete a certain task in a new way? Have they run into any issues they haven't figured out how to solve? Is there anything they don't understand? Did the new process save them as much time as expected?

Showing that you actually *care* about the effectiveness of new solutions, that you value the opinions of people working at your firm, and that you're not thrusting change upon everyone just because, will help everyone at your firm stay engaged and feel valued as more changes and updates are introduced.

The Value of Data

Data is a valuable foundation for decision-making. Once you have some amount of feedback and data to work with, you'll be analyzing it, interpreting results, and making decisions about whether to keep, improve, or scrap certain tools and processes. If the data you have isn't reliable, you won't be making the best possible decisions for your firm—in fact, you could be making key business decisions based on assumptions that aren't true at all.

Feedback from just one client can be incredibly useful. But it isn't fair to take it so far as to assume that their exact experience extends to *all* clients, or even all clients with similar characteristics and life situations. The plural of anecdote is not "data." With more feedback and more data from a representation of your client base that's as broad as possible, you'll have a clearer starting point for discussions on how to improve things at your firm.

Being more data-driven doesn't have to be complicated. When it comes to getting the right amount of data, it's more about having *enough* than it is about having an embarrassment of riches. That's good news, because collecting a lot of feedback from individual customers via complex surveys can be difficult: According to research from survey software company SurveyMonkey, if a survey takes more than seven to eight minutes to complete, the completion rate drops by 5% to 20%.

Only collect as much feedback and data as you can work with and act on. It's better to have a lot of feedback and data on one change you've made to your law firm's client journey—like a new billing format, for example—than to have a huge swath of feedback on more issues than you'd possibly be able to address in a reasonable amount of time.

So what should you measure?

Client Satisfaction Metrics

I've heard from many people within the legal industry that lawyers don't like feedback and that they like the idea of measuring their success even less. For example, when Billie Tarascio of Modern Law started tracking Net Promoter Score (NPS) at her firm—a metric I'll explain later in this section—the lawyers didn't like it. They didn't like being judged, they didn't like being rated, and they came up with all sorts of reasons why they deserved a better rating, or why feedback from certain clients should be ignored. But she persevered and will tell you that tracking NPS is a key part of her firm's success today. The fact is metrics keep us honest. They're useful for any business, including law firms, because they stop us from only looking at favorable anecdotes and positive ratings. Ignoring negative feedback is a dangerous game: If you're not listening to your clients and looking for ways to consistently innovate and improve the client experience, you're standing still in a world where that means being left behind.

The business world has created a variety of metrics for measuring how client-centered your business is, and I've chosen three of them to go over here. Start with one, depending on your firm's goals and your resources for tracking firm metrics, and then review how well it's working. Is the metric being tracked consistently? Are you getting valuable insight that you can act on within your firm?

That said, just as it's important not to be swayed by individual anecdotes, it's also important not to look at an individual metric with blinders on, especially an individual metric at one moment in time. Metrics are important as objective quantitative indicators, but they are just a snapshot. The real value is in how the numbers change over time and in the qualitative feedback underlying the numbers.

A piece of one-off feedback that your new billing process is hard to understand could be just that—a one-off. But if your firm's NPS starts trending down after the implementation of a new billing process, and you start to see a lot more responses mentioning your billing process when clients give feedback as to why they're giving a negative rating, it's worth looking for ways to improve the process.

Finally, it's worth noting that all of the metrics below are used to track customer sentiment in some way, shape, or form, but none are designed specifically to measure the impact of any one change to the client journey. Don't assume causation between any one change and a rise or fall in metrics.

> *The fact is metrics keep us honest. They're useful for any business, including law firms, because they stop us from only looking at favorable anecdotes and positive ratings.*

With that in mind, here are a few ways to measure your success as a client-centered law firm.

NPS (Net Promoter Score)

Net Promoter Score, or NPS, is a metric commonly used to rate customer satisfaction, calculated based on answers to the question "On a scale of 0 to 10, how likely are you to recommend my service to a friend or colleague?" Based on the answer to this question, NPS survey respondents are sorted into Promoters (9 or 10), or people who would actively promote your service; Neutrals (7 or 8), people who wouldn't promote or actively not recommend your product; and Detractors (0 to 6), people who would actively *not* recommend your service.

NPS is calculated by subtracting the percentage of Detractors from the percentage of Promoters to give you an NPS score ranging between -100 to +100. As you may remember from Chapter 1, the NPS for the legal industry overall currently sits at 25, which is in the same range as banks, cell phone companies, and credit card companies.

NPS was introduced by marketing consultant Fred Reicheld in 2003 in a *Harvard Business Review* article, "The One Number You Need to Grow," and has been adopted by many companies, including numerous Fortune 500 companies, since then. NPS has also received its fair share of criticism: There's an inherent assumption that whether or not a client would recommend a company is a good measuring stick for how satisfied a client was with their experience, and not everyone agrees with that assumption. Critics also argue that the survey asks respondents to accurately predict their future behavior (whether they will recommend your product or services to someone), which is difficult to do; or that the way Detractors, Neutrals, and Promoters are bucketed doesn't make sense; or that the method of subtracting the percentage of Detractors from the percentage of Promoters can hide valuable information and lead to big swings in scores.

In my opinion, these criticisms don't discount the usefulness of NPS as a signal to indicate client sentiment, and it's absolutely still worthwhile to use NPS at your firm. It's impossible to distill the entire client experience into a single number, but NPS provides a valuable perspective on your customer's overall sentiment. NPS surveys are also one or two questions long at most, which is important for getting insight in an age where consumers are constantly bombarded with customer satisfaction surveys and don't complete longer ones.

I recommend NPS to firms because it encourages them to ask for feedback, and most importantly, it supports a bias to action, in line with the first and most important value of a client-centered law firm—developing and acting on deep client empathy. It's by being aware of the limitations of NPS (and there will be limitations to *any* broad metric) that you'll get the most out of it.

First, don't look at NPS in a vacuum. Trends matter more than absolute scores (is your NPS going up or down?) and what matters most are the responses to follow-up questions from individual clients. NPS surveys often include a follow-up question asking why clients would or would not recommend a service, and it's here that your firm will find insights you can actually act on. Maybe Promoters love your prompt updates, so you'll know to keep doing those and you can potentially tweak them to make them even better. Maybe your NPS is taking a dive, and when you look at comments from Detractors, you find that most complain that it takes two days to hear back from the firm, which frustrates clients.

Monitor incoming responses for insights, and reach out to detractors quickly. Learn more about what they didn't like about their experience, and act to improve it. By improving the experiences of people who wouldn't mention (or would actively not recommend) your firm, you make for better experiences for future clients, and stem a potential tide of negative reviews.

Beyond that, don't try to "game" your firm's NPS. It can be tempting to ask for feedback at opportune points throughout the client experience or to ask clients for a positive rating (especially if NPS gets formally adopted at your firm and used as a performance metric), but avoiding negative feedback will only make your scores useless. For the same reason, don't cherry-pick happy clients when sending out NPS surveys.

Keep your questions the same, and aim to be consistent with the timing of your NPS surveys: Some companies, including law firms, survey clients multiple times at the same key stages of the customer journey to get an average score that's representative of the client experience. That said, be mindful of how often you're reaching out to clients to ask about NPS, as too many of the same emails will make clients less likely to respond and may even negatively impact their experience.

How to Measure Your NPS

There are multiple tools available to help you track NPS and responses to follow-up questions at your firm. Of course, you could also email out surveys manually and calculate the scores yourself, but I wouldn't recommend it as that approach leaves a lot of room for error and will be time intensive for your staff.

A quick Google search will turn up a wealth of options, but my current favorite is Delighted. It's what we use at Clio. It's relatively easy to set up, and you can receive daily summaries of responses via email. If you use Slack, you can also integrate Slack and Delighted to monitor responses through a Slack channel in real time, which offers great visibility for your entire staff.

CES (Customer Effort Score)

Similar to NPS, Customer Effort Score (CES) is a customer satisfaction metric calculated based on the answer to one question. The difference is it's asked after individual interactions to determine how much effort was put in on the client's part.

CES was created by Matthew Dixon, Karen Freeman, and Nick Toman (Matthew and Nick are two of the authors of *The Effortless Experience*, mentioned earlier in this book). Coincidentally, CES was also introduced and popularized by a *Harvard Business Review* article, entitled "Stop Trying to Delight Your Customers," in 2010. The question used was updated from the original "How much effort did you personally have to put forth to get your issue resolved?" to CES 2.0 in 2013: Customers now agree or disagree on a seven-point scale with the statement "The company made it easy to handle my issue."

Traditionally, CES is used to measure how well a company performs when a customer calls in with a problem, but I'd argue it can also be used to get insight into how much effort clients are putting into any given interaction with your firm. Did your firm make it easy for a client to get an update on their case, fill out a form, sign a document, or pay their bill?

Why or why not? What could you be doing better? What are you doing that makes things easier for clients?

If you're trying to deliver effortless client experiences—which, as a client-centered law firm, you should be doing—this is critical insight to have. However, constantly pinging your clients with surveys does not make their experience more effortless, so you need to find a balance between short-term pain and long-term gain.

It's important not to use CES as a broad-based trending indicator of customer effort. You could take the average of all CES scores as an indicator of how well you're doing, but the authors of *The Effortless Experience* recommend looking at CES scores against a normal distribution (i.e., a bell curve) to look for trends, gaps, and opportunities. Taking an average might mean comparing apples to oranges. For example, if you're an immigration law firm, filling out an incredibly long form will be an inherently higher effort experience for your clients than paying a flat fee online via credit card, so it wouldn't make sense to take an average of scores for those two experiences.

CES is an indicator that helps provide objective insight and should encourage your firm to dig further when opportunities for improvement arise. As with NPS, the real value is in the responses to the follow-up question, "Why?"

How to Measure Your CES

CES surveys are typically sent out after certain types of interactions with a business. For example, you might want to automatically send a CES survey every time a client calls into your firm or logs into your secure client portal for an update. The interactions you want to measure will depend largely on what practice areas your firm covers: The ease of getting updates via a phone call might be more important for family law-focused firms, while the ease of filling out forms might be important for immigration firms, and the ease of reviewing and signing contracts might be more important for firms with corporate clients. It's best to send surveys after a variety of interactions throughout the client experience.

However, as noted above, survey fatigue is real, and too many surveys could lead to a poor experience for your clients. You can stagger surveys by only sending them out at every fifth phone call, for example. As with NPS, there's a smorgasbord of options for measuring CES and helping to automatically send out surveys, such as Surveypal, for example.

CSAT (Customer Satisfaction Score)

The Customer Satisfaction Score (CSAT), which was designed before CES and NPS, is one of the simplest, most fundamental ways to measure the customer experience. A CSAT survey asks variations of the question "How satisfied were you with your experience?" with options to give a rating on a three- to five-point scale. As with CES, CSAT surveys are often sent out immediately after a specific interaction along the client journey, but the question can be asked in the context of one interaction ("How satisfied were you with the response to your question about your case?") or in the context of the client experience as a whole ("How satisfied were you with your experience with our law firm?").

A CSAT question can appear on its own or can be added on to the end of larger client satisfaction surveys. CSAT is calculated by dividing the number of people who say that they were "satisfied" or "very satisfied" by the number of total responses to the survey to give a percentage of satisfied customers. As with NPS and CES, follow-up questions encourage elaboration and can provide valuable insight into why a customer was or was not satisfied with their experience.

Satisfaction might not seem like an exciting metric to measure, but as you'll remember from early chapters, satisfaction is the goal for successful customer-centered businesses. Delighting customers doesn't pay, but keeping your promises and meeting client expectations does. The creators of NPS and CES both found that CSAT was a poor predictor of whether a customer would repurchase a product or service. But it's still useful to look directly at whether customers got what they needed and expected from you, or whether they wanted something more.

How to Measure CSAT

It's recommended to send CSAT surveys out consistently at specific points throughout the client journey, in order to get an accurate picture of the whole client experience. Often, this is done on a rolling basis, so there's a constant stream of feedback to your firm as each client reaches a certain stage. There are plenty of options for tools that will automate CSAT surveys for you, including Delighted, Qualtrics, And Podium.

Leading and Lagging Indicators

As you begin measuring different metrics of success, it's worth knowing the difference between lagging and leading indicators. Lagging indicators measure past success. They can confirm what's already happened, but they can't predict the future. CES and CSAT are examples of lagging indicators: They ask customers how they feel about an interaction that's already happened. Other examples of lagging indicators would be firm revenues or the number of new clients in a given month.

Leading indicators, on the other hand, point to potential signs of future success: They're predictive. For example, if your law firm constantly isn't getting paid on time, you might read that firms who accept credit card payments get paid faster and decide to start accepting credit cards. Monitoring the number of new clients who say they'd like to pay via credit card could be a leading indicator that the payments will be made quicker in the future. NPS is a leading indicator, because it asks clients whether or not they'd recommend you *in the future*. If your most positive clients all really do recommend you, then your firm will grow.

Ideally, it's best to have a mix of leading and lagging indicators when tracking your success. Lagging indicators are more reliable, but leading indicators can help you predict where you're going.

Benchmarking, Analyzing Data, and Interpreting Results

Whether you track NPS, CES, CSAT, or a combination of the three will depend on your goals and on the resources you have available to track and analyze this type of data at your law firm. CES and CSAT look at individual interactions along the client journey, so they're useful for getting insight into whether a change you've made in one spot is having a positive impact. For example, if you streamline your client intake process, you might want to track CES before and after the switch.

NPS, on the other hand, provides more of a 50,000-foot view. It's less useful as an indicator of whether a specific change had an impact, but more useful for illuminating problems you may not have picked up on in your client journey mapping and brainstorming exercises. If you've improved your client intake process, and your CES scores for surveys sent out after client intake are very healthy, but your NPS is going down, it's likely that there's another problem spot in the journey. Look at responses to follow-up questions to help you determine what the issue might be.

Once you've decided what to track, start tracking it as soon as possible, and establish a benchmark. Find this benchmark by looking at what the average NPS, CES, or CSAT is for your firm (or for a given point in the client journey) over two or three months. It will be difficult to tell if a client-centered improvement you've implemented has made a difference if you don't know where you're starting from. For example, ideally, you'd track CES for your client intake process for a few months *before* making a change both to validate that there was an issue in the first place and to see whether the change makes things easier for clients.

A good client experience is critical to your law firm's success, so, if possible, measure both NPS *and* CES or CSAT for a comprehensive look at customer sentiment.

A lot of the value your firm derives from tracking any of the above metrics will come from how you analyze and interpret the results. Get critical about where the numbers are coming from. If your NPS is going up, why is that? Do you have more Promoters or fewer Detractors and more Neutrals?

If there's a sudden spike in positive NPS responses, but there are short responses or no responses at all attached, look a bit more closely before you pat yourself on the back.

This is a good spot to point out that you'll need to be careful if you want to tie employee performance to good NPS or CES scores. Incentivizing good ratings can lead to skewed results without safeguards in place (i.e., staff nudging clients to give positive responses so that they get their bonus), so make it clear that this isn't acceptable and put measures in place to prevent it from happening.

Once you're confident that your numbers are solid, start looking for trends and what they're telling you. If the numbers are going up, look at positive responses so that you know what's going well, and look at negative responses for more opportunities to improve. If the numbers are going down, look for patterns in the negative comments, so that you can prioritize the biggest factor affecting a touchpoint or the overall client experience. Maybe everyone is complaining about billing or, more specifically, the fact that you still send your bills through the mail.

You may want to meet regularly with team members to discuss survey results and potential changes to improve the client experience, but it's also worth having a system for responding to unhappy clients quickly when it makes sense—for example, if a client complains that your hours of operation aren't clearly communicated anywhere on your website, that's an easy fix (and by the way, it'd be worth thanking that customer for her time, because her feedback likely helped your firm improve many other client experiences!).

As a final note, directly measuring client satisfaction is not the only way to tell whether changes at your firm have been successful. You can look at your number of new clients each month, rates of adoption for a new tool, increases in revenue, or staff satisfaction survey results alongside customer satisfaction metrics to confirm that changes in client sentiment are having a material impact. After all, true improvements to the customer experience should eventually yield a positive impact on your bottom line.

So, how do you know that your change project was successful? Any true data analyst, like any true lawyer, will answer, "It depends." In most cases, success will be somewhat subjective. Unless you're carefully designing all new client processes to be implemented perfectly, tracked meticulously, and built to take all possible variables into account, it will be incredibly difficult to definitively show causation, or even correlation.

Rather than looking at the metrics here as proof points, it's better to see them as indicators of success, or as indicators that your firm needs to improve, and nothing more. They're signals that your firm needs to dig deeper and take opportunities to improve the experience it provides.

Act on the feedback your clients provide in their responses to follow-up questions in these surveys, and you'll turn the flywheel of success.

Becoming Data-Driven

Becoming a client-centered law firm also means, to some extent, becoming a data-driven law firm. It means tracking how you're doing and basing your decisions on evidence over hunches and assumptions, whenever possible. The

66 ——

Rather than looking at the metrics here as proof points, it's better to see them as indicators of success, or as indicators that your firm needs to improve, and nothing more. They're signals that your firm needs to dig deeper and take opportunities to improve the experience it provides.

—— 99

importance of being data-driven applies to many areas of your firm—you could track your billable hours logged as a percentage of your total hours worked, as we've spoken about in past *Legal Trends Reports*, for example, to take a good hard look at where your time is going. But being data-driven is most important in the arena of client experience, the one place where getting in line with what your clients really want and need will make or break your firm in an experience-driven world. The client experience is intangible, and getting a definitive measurement is near impossible. But by tracking what you can, looking at indicators of success or trouble, and combing through sentence-form survey responses for opportunities to improve, you'll ensure you have a clearer picture of how your firm is performing and how to continuously innovate.

That said, becoming data-driven shouldn't be overwhelming. While it's ideal to track more than one metric, it's most important to collect data that you can work with and act on. Start small, by tracking *one* thing. Make it call volumes, or online reviews, or the percentage of bills that get paid on time. You can even start by setting up NPS surveys, if you want. Then make one improvement to better that metric, and then another, and then another. As long as you stay focused on improving the client experience, your efforts will lead to more reviews, more referrals, more revenues, and more resources to better track the client experience, so that you can make things better and better. That's how the flywheel turns, and how you'll thrive as a data-driven, client-centered law firm.

13

CLOSING THE LOOP

AS YOU HAVE learned in the last 12 chapters, becoming a client-centered law firm is an ongoing process. No matter how much research, effort, and brainstorming you put into a new system, chances are you won't get it 100% right the first time. Measuring success is part of the equation, but you'll need to analyze the insights you collect, act on them, and get feedback on your new and improved solutions to see if your latest changes were positive. And you'll likely need to do this more than once. Improvement is a circular process, not a linear one. To be successful, you'll need to close the loop by acting on the feedback you receive and the data insights you collect.

A closed loop feedback process is one in which all client feedback and data is acted on in some way. The idea is that no feedback is lost, no client feels unheard, and there's a chance to turn around extremely unhappy clients before they start spreading negative reviews. In the customer service industry, closing the loop is often taken to mean that every client who calls or writes in with feedback receives a response, but the program you implement at your law firm doesn't need to be so intensive. As long as someone is reviewing the feedback and keeping track of it in some way—say, in an Excel data-base—you can ensure any valuable feedback you have isn't going to waste.

Analyzing and acting on feedback will lead to incremental improvements, illuminate new opportunities to improve, and ensure that unhappy clients don't slip through the cracks. In turn, as you implement new iterations of your solutions, your reputation improves, and as you get more positive reviews and referrals, so does your bottom line.

IMPROVEMENT IS A CIRCULAR PROCESS

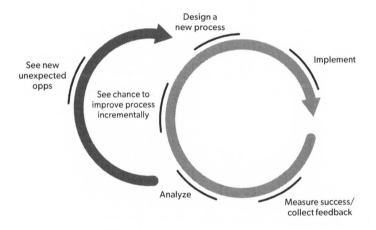

The importance of closing the loop bears out in two ways: responding to feedback from your clients and acting on insights. Both are crucial for creating better client experiences and creating change you can continue to build upon.

Responding to Feedback

Picture this: You purchase some clothes online, and immediately after, you receive one of the NPS surveys that you're constantly inundated with. Normally, you'd click to close the window as fast as you can—because you don't have time to give feedback to the online store selling you shirts—but in this case, you do have some feedback you'd like to share. You loved the selection and prices, but the site was difficult to navigate, and you'd love it if things were a little easier the next time. You respond with a rating of 7 and write up a paragraph explaining what you liked and what could be improved. It's not too long, but you did read it over once to make sure what you had to say was clear. And then you hit send.

And then you never hear back from that site. Ever. Again. Not even in the form of an automated email thanking you for your time. How do you feel? Your time is valuable. You've given up some of it to an entity that you're *paying* for a service so that they can get insights to make *their business* better, and you've been met with silence. Would you shop at that site again? Would you recommend them?

Being open to feedback is important. Actively collecting it is even better. But if you don't respond to your clients and thank them for taking the time to share their thoughts with you, you risk losing a bit of trust in the client relationship and creating a negative experience. This is especially true with clients who provide negative feedback: If you don't respond to them, not only did you provide a negative client experience in the first place, but you've also wasted their time by asking for their feedback and then, in their eyes, not following up on it.

Being open to feedback is important. Actively collecting it is even better. But if you don't respond to your clients and thank them for taking the time to share their thoughts with you, you risk losing a bit of trust in the client relationship and creating a negative experience.

It might be difficult to swallow your pride and open a conversation with a client who's frustrated because you didn't respond as quickly as they would have liked, or you didn't offer payment plans, or they had to fill out the same form twice. But these conversations hold a wealth of opportunity. Not only will you have a chance to get insight into how you might improve the client experience, but you'll also have a chance to turn around (or at least soften) that client's experience—and save yourself a negative review or negative word of mouth.

Making Clients Feel Heard

Making clients feel heard is worth its weight in gold. Of course, you technically can't "make" your clients feel anything, because you can't control their experience. But you *can* do your best to improve their experience by acknowledging their feedback and making it clear that it won't go to waste.

First, thank your clients for taking the time to share their feedback with you. This ties into two of the top values of a client-centered law firm: developing deep client empathy and generating ease through communication. Like you, your clients are human. They won't know whether their feedback has been useful until you tell them. Even if you can't do anything about their issue, either because the moment has passed, or because you can't prioritize that improvement at your firm right away, a simple "I hear you" can go a long way.

Then ask follow-up questions to get more insight into the issue. You might not get a response to that email, but you might open a conversation that could give you a lot of valuable insight. For example, a client might say they hated your client portal, but if you follow up, you might discover that they simply weren't able to log in. It would have been easy to jump to the conclusion that clients didn't like the idea of a portal, and that you should stop using it, when in reality, your instructions on how to access the portal need an update.

These steps are useful even if clients share positive feedback with you, because you can confirm what aspects of the experience your clients liked. This doesn't mean you need to ask for more information from every client who gives you any type of feedback at all, but thanking those who give positive feedback for their time and inviting them to share any further feedback they might have often yields valuable insights that you may not have gotten otherwise.

If you don't have time to personally follow up with every single client, that's okay. Maybe you're a solo lawyer who's already stretched thin, or maybe your firm takes on class action lawsuits with hundreds of clients, so there'll be a *lot* of feedback coming in once you start collecting it. In these cases, you'll need to be more strategic. At the very least, you can send an automated email thanking clients for their feedback and providing a method for them to reach out if they've got more to say (this way, you'll be able to reach out to unhappy clients and try to turn them around before they leave negative reviews), but beyond that, try to reach out to a broad sampling of those who both did and didn't like their experience to give yourself the best overall representation of how your clients think about your services.

Sharing Existing Solutions

Sometimes, the negative feedback clients provide is useful and illuminates a real opportunity—small or large—for your firm to improve the experience it provides. But other times, clients may express their frustration about an issue for which a solution already exists in your firm. For example, maybe a client is upset that she's not able to access information and get new updates on her case, but she's not aware that she could access her case information at any time through your firm's client portal. You provide an overview and all the information needed to log in within your welcome email for new clients, but somehow this got missed.

This type of feedback can be frustrating, but again, making a client feel heard is tremendously valuable, as there's a chance to both solve their issue and figure out where the communication breakdown occurred. If one client missed the login instructions for your client portal, she's likely not the only one—she's the only one who spoke up. Finding out what would have made this information clearer could improve the client experience (and your chances of a positive review) for many other clients down the line.

Making Incremental Improvements

Sometimes, the feedback you get from your clients will highlight big, hairy issues that require time to dig into and tackle, like slow responses and unclear communications at various points throughout a case. But sometimes, a piece of feedback will illuminate an opportunity for a quick fix that could improve the experience for that client (if their case is still ongoing) and/or for many clients that come afterward.

Maybe the consultation form on your firm's website has broken. Maybe you've never claimed your Google My Business profile, so your office hours are missing when clients search for you in Google Maps. Maybe clients are getting calls with simple updates that they would prefer to receive via email. Acting quickly on feedback, fixing small issues, and letting clients know can go a long way toward building good will—when it makes sense to do so.

This doesn't mean you need to implement the exact solutions and fixes that clients suggest. What they say they want isn't always what they actually want: Remember that figuring out their real job to be done in a given situation is how you create an effortless experience for clients and avoid needlessly complicating work at your firm. Even asking one or two follow-up questions to get this insight can go a long way.

More importantly, "quick" fixes aren't always as quick and easy as they seem and not all should be prioritized. There will always be more tweaks, settings, and steps that could be changed and added as part of the way your law firm deals with clients, and it's easier than you may think to get bogged down and lose sight of your long-term plan. These should be the exception, not the rule. Before you make a decision to implement any new changes, prioritize carefully by asking:

- **How much of our client base does this affect?** Will this fix make things better for one client, a small group of clients, or most of your client base?

- **How much investment is required?** How much will it cost to implement the quick fix you're looking at? How much time will it *really* take to set things up differently? Check in with the people who'll be putting change in place—your IT manager, your administrative staff, etc.—before giving the change the okay.

- **How urgent is the issue?** If the phone number on your firm's website is incorrect, or if there's a glitch in your system and clients aren't receiving their bills, those issues need to be fixed right away. If family law clients are feeling anxious about their bills because they're receiving them at a point in the month before they've received their paycheck, shifting your billing period would be a nice fix, but difficult to coordinate, and not something that's important to rush.

Take advantage of opportunities to tweak your process, provide a better client experience, and build trust with clients, but don't let this distract from the larger, more methodical process of implementing, iterating, and slowly creating long-term impactful changes. By thinking carefully about the quick fixes you prioritize, you'll ensure that you're finding a balance and getting a good return on investment on any efforts from your firm.

Planning for the Future

What about those bigger, hairier issues that get pointed out by clients?

Maybe you're trying to get insight into a new communications process with your small business clients, but in their feedback, multiple clients talk about how they wish you were more proactive at asking what else they need help with. They ask if you've ever considered offering a subscription service where you'd regularly check in to ask about ongoing legal needs, rather than depending on the company to call your law firm every time they thought they might need a lawyer. They add that they'd actually be willing to pay more for such a service.

This sounds like an incredible idea for your firm. The only problem is that successfully implementing a subscription service will take careful thought and planning, and you've already prioritized a raft of other client-centered change projects. Throwing this into the mix will be a jarring experience for the hardworking staff and lawyers at your firm—and you've *just* convinced them that the changes that come with shifting to a client-centered approach won't be that bad. But on the other hand, if you can't meet your clients' needs this way, they may very well go to a competitor that will.

The best thing to do in this situation is to plan for it in your firm's future, or put it on your client-centered roadmap and communicate that to your clients. You might not be able to tackle a huge change right at this very moment, but what about next year, or the year after? Even if you can't make a firm commitment, can you put it "in the running"? If you're able to respond to your clients, thank them for their feedback, and let them know that you hear them and you have a plan to address their needs, you'll definitely build their trust, and you might create a client for life.

Better yet, if you can take incremental steps toward implementing a bigger change, you can build goodwill with clients and also experiment with new types of solutions. You might not be able to move to a subscription model immediately, but you could potentially add automated check-in emails, or a simple recurring reminder for you to check in with the clients asking for that kind of attention. It doesn't always have to be all or nothing, and this kind of approach can test the waters for bigger changes.

Just be mindful of how you set expectations. Communicate clearly, and be as honest as you can about the information you have, what types of solutions can be expected, and when. It's better to be realistic up-front than to disappoint down the road.

Acting on Data Insights

If you've responded to your clients and collected some additional feedback, and you're not going to implement a quick fix or put an idea on your long-term roadmap, it's time to get back to the steps to designing a better client experience from Chapter 10. Dig into the data and feedback you've collected, analyze it carefully, and start to define the problem. Is it a communication issue? A tech, process, or implementation problem? Have you misdefined the job to be done at a certain point along the client journey? Or is there more education required to explain to clients why your solution is easier and more efficient for their problem than the solution they might have asked for (e.g., online case updates rather than regular phone calls, meetings, and letters)?

The way you define each subsequent iteration of the problem you're trying to solve will be critical to your continued success as a client-centered firm, because it sets the direction for how you'll improve going forward. Analyze your data and feedback carefully, and try to avoid jumping to any conclusions. Flip back to the "Benchmarking, analyzing data, and interpreting results" section of the last chapter for tips on staying objective.

As a result of the problem you've defined, does the new client-centered change you've implemented need a small tweak? An overall revamp? Does it need to be completely scrapped? Do what you think is needed, but my advice is

66 ——

The way you define each subsequent iteration of the problem you're trying to solve will be critical to your continued success as a client-centered firm, because it sets the direction for how you'll improve going forward.

—— 99

always to lean toward action ahead of over-analysis. The fifth step of designing a better client experience is designing a process *prototype*, not a perfect, be-all end-all solution.

This is similar to the idea of a minimum viable product (MVP) talked about in tech circles: There's much more value put on testing versus getting everything right the first time. After all, you can't read your clients' minds, so you do need to get it in front of them before you can know whether you've done the right thing and improved the client experience.

On Anecdotal Feedback

It's important to look objectively at overall feedback, data, and trends regarding the client experience at your law firm, rather than being swayed by a few vocal clients. While it's important to respond to feedback from those who provide it, it's equally important not to conflate those opinions with the opinions of your broader client base: You might miss valuable nuances or head in the wrong direction entirely.

That said, there *will* be moments where it makes sense to act on anecdotal feedback at your law firm. After all, don't forget that one client can often speak for many more who couldn't take the time or were too nervous to say it themselves. If someone says your bills are hard to read, that's not *just* one person saying that—that's the one person who bothered.

Beyond feedback, there's a school of thought that Big Data isn't the only way to get meaningful insight, and that getting more detailed feedback from a few clients can also be valuable. In his book *Small Data*, Martin Lindstrom talks about how he spends his time observing small groups of consumers closely, rather than poring over spreadsheets, to unlock useful information about what people really want. This is useful news if, as a law firm, your capacity for collecting feedback is more along the lines of surveys and interviews than mass data collection. If you pay close attention, there's a lot to be learned from anecdotes.

There are a few cases in which acting on anecdotal feedback has worked for us at Clio. On September 6, 2018, a lawyer using Clio asked us on Twitter why the Global Create button—which lets you create new time entries, calendar events, and more from anywhere within the program—didn't then have the option to create a task (i.e., a to-do item). This sparked a wave of discussion within our design and development teams. Four days later, we were able to tweet back that one of our developers had updated the Global Create button based on his question. We were able to build goodwill with that one customer and also make a change that would conceivably have a positive impact on all other Clio customers.

Now, of course it wouldn't make sense to act on *every* suggestion that comes in off the cuff via Twitter, Facebook, email, or other channels. Not all issues are as clear-cut. Also, we depend on a broad sampling of customer feedback to create cohesive, long-term plans to continuously improve Clio, and it's important not to deprioritize the inputs of many customers in favor of the voice of one. But sometimes, every once in a while, that one voice says something that just makes sense, and that somehow wasn't brought up in any previous feedback, so it's only natural for us to act on it.

The circumstances that dictate when, how often, and even if you choose to act on anecdotal feedback over longer-term trends and data insights at your firm will depend on the practice areas you work in, the size of your firm, and the general level of acceptance for more client-centered processes at your firm, among other things. For example, for a firm with fewer resources to devote to client-centered change projects, serving customers used to very specific processes, staffed by lawyers and administrative assistants who are hesitant about implementing any client-centered change in the first place, it may not be the best idea to throw one-off changes in response to anecdotal feedback into the mix. But for a firm where leadership is open to the idea of constantly iterating on processes to provide better client experiences, once there's a solid foundation of overall client feedback to provide context, acting on anecdotal feedback over carefully considered insights might be okay once in a blue moon.

Again, quick fixes and responses to individual pieces of anecdotal feedback should be the exception, not the rule. Whenever possible, follow the steps outlined in Chapter 10 to ensure you're staying true to designing the client journey to create effortless experiences. Keep this in mind as you continue to measure your success and act on feedback, and you'll ensure that you close the loop rather than going off on a tangent. The changes you make must accurately meet client needs, while making your internal processes more efficient.

Implementing Change, Again

Change can be tough to manage, in more ways than one. How soon, after implementing a new, carefully considered client-centered process, should you introduce more change? This is where you'll want to be careful. Too much change, introduced all at once, and especially with a lack of clarity about why so much change is coming so soon, can lead to confusion or loss of trust in the process. Also, it's important to wait to see the impact of your changes before jumping to the conclusion that further change is needed. It's easier than ever to make assumptions when you've just launched a new client intake form, a billing format, or onboarding document: You'll think of something the moment you put it out to the world. But let it rest (unless it's a typo). Wait a few weeks or months to see whether clients stop asking the same questions about your intake or billing processes—or whether new processes pop up in their place. You might save yourself a lot of back and forth.

Also, remember that communication is crucial when you're launching yet another change, for both staff and lawyers at your firm and your clients. Make sure everyone gets a heads up *before* the latest way of doing things is made official (and after, but we'll discuss that in a minute). Be clear about what's changing and how it affects different groups, and make the message only as long as it needs to be. Generate ease through communication.

There's no need to overdo it. If it's a small change, even a quick message highlighting that everyone might notice there's a small change to your client intake form (and explaining why) would be appropriate. If it's a larger change, take a quick read through the principles of change management outlined in Chapter 11 to ensure you're set up to roll out your latest change successfully.

The better you get at implementing and communicating change well, the more you build trust within your law firm, meaning less friction and more freedom to make small tweaks to create better and better client experiences.

Measuring, Again

Once you've listened to feedback, brainstormed new solutions, and tweaked your process or implemented something new accordingly, there's one last step: You'll need to measure the success of your latest iteration in order to truly close the loop.

There are a few different ways to do this. You could use CES and CSAT to gauge client ease and satisfaction with your new process. You could also see if the dates of any changes coincide with a notable change in your firm's NPS. Likely, the most important thing you can do is to read the sentence-form responses to the surveys to get further feedback for improvement and confirmation about what parts of your tool or process work best. But a number, as long as it's not treated as the be-all end-all indicator, can provide a clear and easy-to-understand indicator of success to rally the team around.

Don't forget to collect feedback from your staff and colleagues as well. Likely, many of the changes you implement will directly affect the people you work with. In fact, if there's a lot of behind-the-scenes work to make a certain piece of the client experience more effortless, changes likely affect your staff and colleagues *more* than your clients. Ask everyone how they think the latest tweak is going, and keep an open mind.

In addition to directly measuring client sentiment with metrics like NPS and CES, there are other ways to measure the success of your client-centered initiatives. For example, maybe only 50% of your clients have ever logged into your firm's client portal to access their own case information, but you were hoping that this number would be upward of 80%. You could keep track of the percentage of clients logging into your client portal, and watch to see whether it goes up or down following small changes to the process. Changes might mean an updated welcome email with better instructions, or asking attorneys to suggest that clients use the portal instead of calling into the firm. Even better, you could track the volume of emails and phone calls your firm receives and needs to respond to, and check whether these numbers go down as improvements are put in place and clients use other tech tools to communicate with the firm. Whatever you do, keep objectively measuring how changes to the way your firm operates improve the client experience, and you'll be on the right track.

Finally, keep sharing ongoing findings and feedback with your staff to keep everyone engaged with the process. You're introducing a lot of new change at your firm, and sticking to a set cadence of implementing, testing, analyzing feedback, updating, and implementing again can help create trust in the process and keep ideas top-of-mind. Keeping lawyers and staff informed can also invite further conversations and suggestions, and you never know—someone might have a home-run idea that helps your firm stand out from the competition like never before.

Closing the Loop and Turning the Flywheel

As we're reaching the end of a book on how to run a client-centered law firm, it would be easy to assume that this is the last step in the process. Of course, this isn't the case. The act of closing the loop is just the beginning: It lays out the framework for a continuous process of improvement at your firm.

More important than any tactical change to improve the client experience is an underlying shift to a client-centered mindset in your firm. It's with this mindset that innovative thinkers can thrive at your firm and introduce improvements to the experiences of law firm staff and clients alike. Once a loop of implementing change, testing, assessing, brainstorming, implementing, and testing again is in motion, every cycle helps reduce friction or barriers to change. With every success comes acceptance. Every time the effort needed to complete a task gets reduced, or a client calls in and is more pleasant on the phone, or your firm receives a positive review for your excellent service, staff and lawyers will get a bit more used to the idea of constant iteration as the new normal.

Sure, you might experience a few flops, receive a few eyerolls, and hear a few claims that any "failure" means that the firm should give up on this new mindset altogether. But as I've mentioned in earlier chapters, the processes and innovations in this book are not bleeding-edge technologies in ethically murky waters. They're entirely fair game, so the likelihood of any risk that would pose an existential threat to the firm is slim. If anything, going through a less-than-successful process change will be equally as valuable as going through a successful one, because it shows everyone that things can shift from the traditional law firm model and not go according to plan and still be okay—as long as the firm learns from the experience and keeps moving forward.

Keep the flywheel effect in mind, and be patient but persistent. If you can continue to put in a sustained effort to make improvements at your firm, the flywheel effect will kick into action, setting you on a path to get more reviews, more referrals, more new clients, and more revenues. And staff and lawyers will enjoy more efficient processes, a more pleasant work environment, and for the lawyers, more time to do what they went to law school for.

I've provided some scaffolding and some basic tools to empower lawyers and legal professionals to build more client-centered firms, but my hope is that you'll take these principles and processes and iterate on those as well. Make them your own, use them to build the most successful client-centered firm you can, and pass them on to friends and colleagues in the industry so that they can do the same. This is the flywheel effect in action for the whole legal industry. Before you know it, law firms will be thriving like never before, more and more people will have access to legal services, and the entire legal system will be more effective for everyone.

Conclusion

THE LAW FIRM
OF THE FUTURE

IN *The Future of the Professions*, Richard and Daniel Susskind talk about the idea of a Grand Bargain made between professionals and the rest of society. Under the terms of the bargain, professionals get to provide a service, often to the exclusion of all others. They also get to self-regulate and enjoy relative respect and prestige. In return, they set a high bar for entry into the profession, maintain their expertise, and act honestly and in the best interests of clients.

Richard and Daniel argue that, due to the advent of technology and a general lack of affordability for professional services, the general public no longer agrees to this deal, and they predict that the professions will look very different in the future compared to how they look today. I'd agree with that sentiment: Acting in the best interests of clients should extend to fair pricing and a reasonably navigable legal experience, because these factors are intertwined with whether or not someone can get access to justice—or access to legal services—in the first place. If you can't afford a lawyer, or the way the legal experience has been designed makes it prohibitively difficult and stressful to even attempt to solve your issue by hiring a lawyer, then there absolutely needs to be another way.

What will the law firm of the future look like? The answer to that question is largely up to people like you, the lawyers and legal professionals working in law firms today. Whether the innovative law firms of the future borrow from the models of alternative legal service providers, or whether they come up with something entirely different, is up to them.

My prediction, however, is that successful law firms of the future will embrace change as a constant state, rather than as a risk to be avoided, or even as something temporary that's needed to get to a new normal. Embracing change and responding to the world around you is critical to the success of a client-centered law firm. If you listen to your clients and invest in change for a little while, you only turn your firm's flywheel of success a few times, and it'll eventually slow to a stop. But if you commit to staying open to change, and you keep putting effort in to iterate on the way your firm operates, your flywheel will only spin faster and faster, and you'll thrive in the modern era of law firms.

If you're a lawyer, this doesn't mean you need to abandon the practice of law and focus on becoming a tech-savvy, client-centered legal entrepreneur. Far from it. It's the little changes that matter. Small changes that stick are much better than flashy ideas that make a big splash but that staff fail to adopt, or that clients point out a plethora of new issues with. Start with what you can, and build a habit of taking feedback, analyzing, brainstorming, implementing, and measuring. Sooner than you think, you'll have created more efficient processes that give you *more* time to focus on practicing law.

As mentioned throughout the book, the concept of client-centered lawyering, or running a client-centered law firm, is nothing new. Leading thinkers like Jordan Furlong have written about it. Leading legal websites have published articles about it. Innovative firms like Ziva Law even have "client-centered service" highlighted as a key piece of the value they provide on the homepage of their website. But so far, we still haven't seen a broad uptake of client-centered practices in the legal industry. What law firms offer, for the most part, still doesn't match what clients need, and closing that gap is becoming more and more important for law firms that want to stay competitive in the experience-driven era. I hope that, for you, this book has made clear the need to act now and has given you a manual for how to put those ideas into action. The frameworks provided should provide a solid starting point to get a loop of client-centered change up and running.

If your firm can successfully adopt a client-centered mindset, and consistently create increasingly client-centered experiences, you'll build a strong reputation and get more reviews, more referrals, and more new business. And lawyers and staff will be happier, to boot. The best part is the ability to adapt and change is transferable, no matter what direction the legal industry heads in. If virtual reality becomes even more mainstream than it already is, and starts to affect professional services as well, for example, you'll be ready to pivot and thrive in that environment with the skills you've learned here. As long as you maintain a relentless focus on the client experience, and a constant openness to change, your firm will be able to handle anything that comes its way.

But this isn't just about your firm, or any one firm for that matter. There's potential to grow the entire legal industry by accessing latent demand in the legal market with a client-centered approach. For lawyers, legal professionals, and law firms that feel they're not thriving, not making what they're worth, or not making the difference they hoped to make when they got into this field, there's a huge opportunity to change that, here and now. But it needs to start with you.

So I ask of you this: No matter how you can start to make a difference and create a client-centered shift in the legal industry, start today. Introduce a colleague to the idea of the client experience. Ask a client if they understand billing processes at your firm, or if they'd prefer different payment options. Start tracking your own NPS, even if you can't implement NPS tracking across your entire firm. It all counts.

The weight of the flywheel for the entire legal industry is immense, and cumulatively, it will take a momentous amount of effort before the wheel starts spinning at full speed. In the moment, the small change you make might seem difficult, and it might not feel like it's making a difference at all. But really, what is a giant push but the slow accumulation of a million smaller ones?

What you do matters, and it matters in a big way. You have the tools you need to drive change. The future of the legal profession—and your clients—depend on you to use them.

GLOSSARY

Alternative Legal Service Provider (ALSP): A company or organization that packages and provides legal services differently from traditional law firms. This can mean unbundled services, subscription services, or any other number of innovative practices.

Client-centered law firm: A law firm that puts its clients at the center of all of its decision-making and ensures internal efficiency in all new processes.

Client experience: How a client thinks and feels about your firm as a result of their experiences with you.

Client journey: The sum of all of a client's touchpoints along their legal journey, both with your firm and beyond. Often, the client journey starts well before a client first contacts your firm.

Client journey map: A visualization of the client experience, including various touchpoints and the client's thoughts, feelings, and actions at each point in time throughout their experience. This likely includes experiences beyond those directly involving your organization.

Client lifecycle: The idea that the client journey is not linear but circular, as clients may use the services of a law firm again at a future time after their initial case has concluded.

Closed loop feedback: A system in which every piece of feedback from clients is acted on in some way, whether by following up with a client for additional information, or by simply acknowledging and reviewing that feedback and adding it into the firm's database.

Customer Effort Score (CES): A metric used to track how easy or difficult it was for a client to get their issue resolved. May also be used to measure how easy or difficult it was for a client to complete a task or accomplish a certain goal, e.g., to fill out a client intake form or get an update on a legal case.

Customer Satisfaction Score (CSAT): A metric that measures customer satisfaction with regard to discrete experiences along the client journey, using responses to variations on the question "How satisfied were you with your experience?"

Design thinking: A problem-solving mindset often employed by professional designers that prioritizes understanding customer needs and deters jumping to conclusions. Design thinking emphasizes thoughtful customer research, a clear definition of the problem to be solved, and the brainstorming of a variety of solutions before settling on one to move forward with.

The flywheel effect: Coined by Jim Collins, author of *Good to Great*, the flywheel effect describes how sustained efforts over a long period of time can eventually kick off an unstoppable momentum that takes businesses from good to great.

Gartner Hype Cycle: A visualization created by research and advisory company Gartner to help investors think through the benefits and risks of new technologies over time. Key stages include the Innovation Trigger, the Peak of Inflated

Expectations, the Trough of Disillusionment, the Slope of Enlightenment, and the Trough of Productivity.

Jobs to be Done theory: Created by Harvard Business School professor Clayton Christensen, it is the idea that clients, customers, and users don't buy products, they "hire" solutions for their "jobs to be done," and that organizations can become successful by tailoring their products or services to the jobs their clients are trying to get done.

Lagging indicator: A measure of outputs that indicate past performance, such as past quarter revenues.

Leading indicator: A measure of something that might predict future success. For example, the number of clients who say they'd recommend you might predict future growth.

Net Promoter Score (NPS): A metric commonly used to rate customer satisfaction, calculated based on answers to the question "On a scale of 0 to 10, how likely are you to recommend my services to a friend or colleague?"

Process prototype: An early model of a new client-centered process to be tested on a small scale before being implemented widely at your firm.

Touchpoint: A single point along the client journey where an organization interacts with a client.

ACKNOWLEDGMENTS

THIS BOOK COULD not have come together without the help of a great number of people from within Clio and beyond. First on that list is the community of lawyers around us who are transforming the practice of law, for good. We have the privilege of working with some of the best law firms in the world, not only as a software provider but as a partner in what the future of law firms will look like. I'd like to extend a special thank-you to the lawyers and firms doing the amazing client-centered work showcased in this book: Patrick Palace and Jordan Couch of Palace Law, Greg McLawsen of Sound Immigration, Nicholas Hite of The Hite Law Group, Jason Golbey of Golbey Law, Katy Young of Ad Astra Law Group, Billie Tarascio of Modern Law, everyone at Cascade Legal Planning, Locks Law Firm, and Ziva Law, and Catherine Merino Reisman, Clio's first customer. We are honored to have earned the trust of the many lawyers and legal professionals who use Clio and to contribute to the success of the legal industry with them.

Clio is where it is today, and I have had the opportunity to write this book, thanks to the support of these customers and those who've invested in and championed Clio since the beginning. To our close friends and family who took a chance on Clio, to our friend at the Law Society of British Columbia whose insight into the challenges of small law firms inspired the initial creation of Clio Manage, and to our valued past and present investors, including Christoph Janz of Point Nine Capital, Boris Wertz, formerly of Acton Capital Partners, now founder and general partner at Version One Ventures, Bessemer Venture Partners, and now to TCV and JMI Equity— thank you for your support in growing this company and in our mission to improve the day-to-day of lawyers and legal professionals.

I'm also incredibly grateful to legal industry veterans Bob Ambrogi and Kevin O'Keefe, who rooted for us from day one and who've welcomed us into long-running discussions on how to innovate and evolve the practice of law. Other leading legal thinkers who've provided inspiration for this book include Jordan Furlong, whose writing on how law is becoming a buyer's market is a critical contribution to the client-centered shift in the legal industry; Matt Homann, who's always challenged the norms of the legal industry and held a client-centered view; and Richard Susskind, who's written extensively on the need for lawyers to be aware of coming change in the legal industry. There are also Ed Walters, Joshua Kubicki, Margaret Hagan, Cat Moon, Jeena Cho, Michele DeStefano, John Suh, Heidi Gardner, Jay Foonberg, Mark Cohen, Kimberly Y. Bennett, Erin Levine, Jess Birken, and far too many others to name here. My hope is that this book is a valuable addition to their outstanding work, which is already stoking change in the industry.

Then there are the leading thinkers from beyond the world of legal whose ideas this book draws on for support: Jim Collins, Matthew Dixon, Nick Toman, Karen Freeman, Rick DeLisi, Fred Reichheld, Clayton Christensen, Jeffrey Liker, Carol Dweck, Gartner, IDEO, and the many designers who've contributed to discussions on design thinking. In particular, I'd like to thank Tony Hsieh: I met Tony on a visit to Zappos' offices in 2009, and his customer obsession has inspired much of my personal business philosophy today.

I'd also like to thank the members of the Clio team who helped make this book a reality: Teresa Matich and Erin Walker, for your help organizing my thoughts and guiding me in crafting a piece that's both compelling and useful, and Joshua Lenon, for your help with the research for this book. I'm also grateful to Carina Hunt, Karen Whistler, Alex Mak, Marc Dyer, and many other Clio team members who shared their expertise to make this book as rich and helpful as possible.

And of course, I'd like to thank my lifelong friend and cofounder, Rian Gauvreau. Thank you for your commitment to building the human and high-performing culture that's at the heart of Clio's success today.

Finally, neither this book nor Clio would be where it is today without the endless love and support from my wife, Tonia, and our three children, Ian, Patrick, and Isla. Thank you for your enduring patience and your continued willingness to say yes to this adventure.

NOTES

INTRODUCTION

"90% of startups failing": Erin Griffith, "Why Startups Fail, According to Their Founders," *Fortune*, September 25, 2014, fortune.com/2014/09/25/why-startups-fail-according-to-their-founders.

CHAPTER 1

"Joshua Kubicki, cofounder of Bold Duck Studio": Greg McLawsen and Joshua Kubicki, "Why the Client Experience Matters," in *Matters: A Podcast from Clio*, produced by Andrew Booth, Teresa Matich, Sam Rosenthal, and Derek Bolen, podcast, 30:13, clio.com/podcast/why-client-experience-matters.

"Starbucks is the world's largest coffee chain": Barclay Palmer, "The World's 10 Biggest Restaurant Companies," *Investopedia*, June 23, 2019, investopedia.com/articles/markets/012516/worlds-top-10-restaurant-companies-mcdsbux.asp.

"27,000 locations in more than 76 countries worldwide": John Levesque, "How Many Starbucks Stores Are There Worldwide?" *Seattle Business*, September 2018, seattlebusinessmag.com/business-operations/how-many-starbucks-stores-are-there-worldwide.

"the PwC Future of Customer Experience survey": David Clarke and Ron Kinghorn, "Experience Is Everything," PwC, 2018, pwc.com/future-of-cx.

"with over 150 million subscribers globally": Netflix, Inc., *United States Securities and Exchange Commission form 10-Q*, period ending June 30, 2019, page 19.

"more than 6 million Airbnb listings worldwide": Jaleesa Bustamante, "Airbnb Statistics," iProperty Management, October 2019, ipropertymanagement.com/airbnb-statistics.

"Uber is now available in 700 cities": "Find Uber in Cities Around the World," Uber Technologies, Inc., 2019, uber.com/global/en/cities.

"14 million Uber trips are taken every day": Mansoor Iqbal, "Uber Revenue and Usage Statistics," *Business of Apps*, May 10, 2019, businessofapps. com/data/uber-statistics.

"*The Effortless Experience*": Matthew Dixon, Nick Toman, and Rick Delisi, *The Effortless Experience: Conquering the New Battleground for Customer Loyalty* (Portfolio, 2013).

"Many cities issue a limited number of medallions": Ian Cameron, "Municipalities Limit Number of Taxi Medallions," *Times Colonist*, April 17, 2016, timescolonist.com/opinion/letters/ municipalities-limit-number-of-taxi-medallions-1.2232857.

"Many have taken to the streets": "Anti-Uber Protests Around the World, in Pictures," *The Telegraph*, undated, telegraph.co.uk/technology/ picture-galleries/11902080/Anti-Uber-protests-around-the-world- in-pictures.html.

"*Law Is a Buyer's Market*": Jordan Furlong, *Law Is a Buyer's Market: Building a Client-First Law Firm* (Law21 Press, 2017).

"Joshua Browder's DoNotPay bot": John Mannes, "DoNotPay Launches 1,000 New Bots to Help You with Your Legal Problems," *Tech Crunch*, July 12, 2017, techcrunch.com/2017/07/12/donotpay-launches-1000- new-bots-to-help-you-with-your-legal-problems.

"you can also use it to sue": Jon Porter, "Robot Lawyer DoNotPay Now Lets You 'Sue Anyone' via an App," *The Verge*, October 18, 2018, theverge.com/2018/10/10/17959874/ donotpay-do-not-pay-robot-lawyer-ios-app-joshua-browder.

"*Legal Upheaval*": Michele DeStefano, *Legal Upheaval: A Guide to Creativity, Collaboration, and Innovation in Law* (American Bar Association, 2018).

"Premonition is a tool": Premonition (website), premonition.ai.

"Clio's *2018 Legal Trends Report* analyzed": Clio, *Legal Trends Report* (2018), clio.com/resources/legal-trends/2018-report.

"a report from the World Justice Project": World Justice Project, *Global Insights on Access to Justice: Findings from the World Justice Project General Population Poll in 45 Countries* (2018), worldjusticeproject. org/sites/default/files/documents/WJP_Access-Justice_January_2018_ LR_0.pdf.

"An overwhelming 86% of consumers": Oracle, *2011 Customer Experience Impact Report: Getting to the Heart of the Consumer and Brand Relationship* (2011), oracle.com/us/products/applications/cust-exp- impact-report-epss-1560493.pdf.

"Adobe's *2018 Digital Trends* report": Prateek Vatash, *Digital Intelligence Briefing: 2018 Digital Trends* (Econsultancy and Adobe, 2018), adobe. com/content/dam/acom/en/modal-offers/pdfs/0060629.en.aec. whitepaper.econsultancy-2018-digital-trends-US.pdf.

"Nearly two-thirds (61%) of consumers": Adobe; Goldsmiths, University of London; and Smoothmedia; *Reinventing Loyalty: Understanding Consumer Behaviour in the Experience Era* (Adobe, 2017), blogs.adobe.com/digitaleurope/files/2017/09/ Adobe-Goldsmiths-Reinventing-Loyalty- Report4.pdf.

"According to RightNow's *Customer Experience Impact Report*": RightNow Technologies, *Customer Experience Impact Report 2010* (October 9, 2010), slideshare.net/RightNow/2010-customer-experience-impact.

CHAPTER 2

"Blockbuster went bankrupt in 2010": Greg Satell, "A Look Back at Why Blockbuster Really Failed and Why It Didn't Have To," *Forbes*, September 5, 2014, forbes.com/sites/gregsatell/2014/09/05/a-look- back-at-why-blockbuster-really-failed-and-why-it-didnt-have-to.

"Netflix's revenues were sitting around $2 billion": Macrotrends, "Netflix Revenue 2006-2019 | NFLX," accessed November 6, 2019, macrotrends.net/stocks/charts/NFLX/netflix/revenue.

"the roughly $6 billion in revenue": Christopher Harress, "The Sad End of Blockbuster Video," *International Business Times*, December 5, 2013, ibtimes.com/sad-end-blockbuster-video-onetime-5-billion-company- being-liquidated-competition-1496962.

"average number of trips taken per day": Todd W. Schneider, "Taxi and Ridehailing Usage in New York City," accessed November 5, 2019, toddwschneider.com/dashboards/nyc-taxi-ridehailing-uber-lyft-data.

"Demand has continued to grow": "3 Charts Showing Growth of Short- Term Rentals vs. Hotel Online Bookings," Travel Data Daily, undated, traveldatadaily.com/charts-short-term-vs-hotel-booking.

"By 2017, Airbnb's 4 million listings": Avery Hartmans, "Airbnb Now Has More Listings Worldwide than the Top Five Hotel Brands Combined," *Business Insider*, August 10, 2017, businessinsider.com/ airbnb-total-worldwide-listings-2017-8.

"*The Future of Law*": Richard Susskind, *The Future of Law: Facing the Challenges of Information Technology* (Oxford University Press, 1996).

"In 2001, a business writer for the *Denver Post*": Anne Colden, "Self-help Law Customers Courted," *Denver Post*, February 12, 2001, extras. denverpost.com/business/biz0212d.htm.

"the Texas Legislature exempted": Nolo, "The Brief Story of Texas vs. Nolo," *Nolo's Blog*, April 11, 2011, blog.nolo.com/blog/2011/04/11/the-brief-story-of-texas-vs-nolo.

"Thomas D. Russell": Doreen Carvajal, "Lawyers Are Not Amused by Feisty Legal Publisher," *The New York Times*, August 24, 1998, nytimes.com/1998/08/24/business/lawyers-are-not-amused-by-feisty-legal-publisher.html.

"Only 44% of people would seek a lawyer": Neil Rose, "When Is a Problem a Legal Problem?" *The Guardian*, June 22, 2010, theguardian.com/law/2010/jun/22/recognising-legal-problems-as-legal.

"As of 2016, the size of the US legal market": Thomson Reuters, "How Big Is the U.S. Legal Services Market?" (2015), legalexecutiveinstitute.com/wp-content/uploads/2016/01/How-Big-is-the-US-Legal-Services-Market.pdf.

"demand for legal services grew 1.3% in 2018": Thomson Reuters, "Rebuilding the Law Firm Model: 2019 Report on the State of the Legal Market" From Georgetown Law and Thomson Reuters Legal Executive Institute," news release, January 9, 2019, https://images.ask.legalsolutions.thomsonreuters.com/Web/TRlegalUS/%7B7f73da9c-0789-4f63-b012-379d45d54cdf%7D_2019_Report_on_the_State_of_the_Legal_Market_NEW.pdf.

"almost 40% of Americans couldn't cover an unexpected expense of $400": Board of Governors of the Federal Reserve System, *Report on the Economic Well-Being of U.S. Households in 2018* (May 2019), federalreserve.gov/publications/files/2018-report-economic-well-being-us-households-201905.pdf.

"Take *The Atlantic*": Lauren Indvik, "Inside 'The Atlantic,'" *Mashable*, December 19, 2011, mashable.com/2011/12/19/the-atlantic-digital-first.

"that number had risen to 42.3 million": *The Atlantic*, "The Atlantic Reaches Record Audience of 42.3 Million in May 2017," news release, June 1, 2017, theatlantic.com/press-releases/archive/2017/06/the-atlantic-reaches-record-audience-in-may-2017/528798.

"*The Atlantic* was profitable again": Lucia Moses, "How David Bradley and Justin Smith Saved 'The Atlantic,'" *Adweek*, September 27, 2011, adweek.com/digital/how-david-bradley-and-justin-smith-saved-atlantic-135215.

"one of the top 50 news sites": Alexa Internet, Inc., "The Top 500 Sites on the Web: By Category," accessed November 5, 2019, alexa.com/topsites/category/News.

"a total circulation of 474,274 subscriptions": Alliance for Audited Media, "Consumer Magazines: Total Circulation," data for period ending June 30, 2019, abcas3.auditedmedia.com/ecirc/magtitlesearch.asp.

"Jordan Furlong mentioned *The Atlantic* story": Jordan Furlong, "How to Kill a Law Firm," *The Law21 Blog*, August 12, 2010, law21.ca/2010/08/how-to-kill-a-law-firm.

"the following quote from Justin Smith": Bill Mickey, "Behind *The Atlantic*'s Brand Reinvention," *Folio*, June 9, 2010, foliomag.com/behind-atlantics-brand-reinvention.

"Take Aldi, for example": Nathaniel Meyersohn, "How a Cheap, Brutally Efficient Grocery Chain Is Upending America's Supermarkets," CNN *Business*, May 17, 2019, edition.cnn.com/interactive/2019/05/business/aldi-walmart-low-food-prices/index.html.

"1,400 items, compared to a typical 40,000": Tara Bozick, "Second Aldi in Newport News Opens with Fanfare," *Daily Press*, April 27, 2017, dailypress.com/business/tidewater/dp-tidewaterbiz-aldi-20170427-story.html.

"its competitors have struggled": David Nicklaus, "Save-A-Lot Owner Will Probably Take a Loss on Struggling Grocery Chain," *St. Louis Post-Dispatch*, May 12, 2019, stltoday.com/business/columns/david-nicklaus/save-a-lot-owner-will-probably-take-a-loss-on/article_703b627c-e87b-510b-b831-28cdab3c9e61.html.

"the world's eighth largest retailer by revenue": Deloitte, *Global Powers of Retailing 2019* (2019), deloitte.com/content/dam/Deloitte/global/Documents/Consumer-Business/cons-global-powers-retailing-2019.pdf.

"DLA Piper": DLA Piper, "DLA Piper named by the Financial Times as one of the top ten Most Innovative Law firms in North America for both the Business of Law and Legal Expertise," news release, December 11, 2018, dlapiper.com/en/canada/news/2018/12/dla-piper-named-by-the-financial-times; DLA Piper, "DLA Piper named one of the most innovative law firms in Europe by the Financial Times Innovative Lawyers Europe Report 2017," news release, October 6, 2017, dlapiper.com/en/us/news/2017/10/dla-piper-one-of-the-most-innovative-law-firms.

"the firm's Accelerate website": DLA Piper, "Accelerate" (website), dlapiperaccelerate.com.

"Ascendant 2.0": DLA Piper, "Ascendant 2.0" (website), ascendant. dlapiper.com.

"PatBot": Artificial Lawyer, "Meet PatBot — The New Personal Injury Legal Bot by LawDroid," May 15, 2018, artificiallawyer.com/2018/05/15/ meet-patbot-the-new-personal-injury-legal-bot-by-lawdroid.

CHAPTER 3

"You can now see a doctor via video": Artificial Lawyer, "Meet PatBot — The New Personal Injury Legal Bot by LawDroid," May 15, 2018, artificiallawyer.com/2018/05/15/ meet-patbot-the-new-personal-injury-legal-bot-by-lawdroid.

"Comment 8 to Rule 1.1 of the ABA's Model Rules of Professional Conduct": Robert J. Ambrogi, "Tech Competence," *LawSites*, accessed November 5, 2019, lawsitesblog.com/tech-competence.

"37 US states have adopted the revised comment": Robert J. Ambrogi, "Tech Competence," *LawSites*, accessed November 5, 2019, lawsitesblog.com/tech-competence.

"our very first customer, Catherine Merino Reisman": Clio, "Clio's First Customer: How Catherine Merino Reisman Has Grown Over 10 Years," undated, clio.com/customers/clios-first-customer-how-catherine-merino-reisman-has-grown-over-10-years.

"ABA's 2018 *TECHREPORT*": Dennis Kennedy, "TechReport 2018: Cloud Computing," *Law Technology Today*, January 14, 2019, lawtechnologytoday.org/2019/01/techreport-2018-cloud-computing.

"94% of organizations using the cloud": Flexera, "Cloud Computing Trends: 2019 State of the Cloud Survey," Flexera blog, February 27, 2019, blogs.flexera.com/cloud/cloud-industry-insights/ cloud-computing-trends-2019-state-of-the-cloud-survey.

"revenues for ALSPs grew": Center on Ethics and the Legal Profession at Georgetown Law, Thomson Reuters Legal Executive Institute, Professional Service Firms (PSF) Group at Saïd Business School, University of Oxford, and Acritas, *Alternative Legal Service Providers 2019: Fast Growth, Expanding Use and Increasing Opportunity* (2019), legal.thomsonreuters.com/content/dam/ewp-m/documents/legal/en/ pdf/reports/alsp-report-final.pdf.

"Axiom": Hannah Roberts, "Axiom to Go Public, Applying for IPO and Spinning Off Two Businesses," Law.com, February 19, 2019, https:// www.businesswire.com/news/home/20190219005611/en/ Knowable-Axiom-Managed-Solutions-Spun-Axiom https://www.permira.com/news-views/news/permira-funds-complete-investment-in-axiom/.

"UnitedLex": Hamish McNicol, "New Law Leader UnitedLex Targets Rapid Expansion after Acquisition by PE Heavyweight CVC," *Legal Business*, September 21, 2018, legalbusiness.co.uk/blogs/ new-law-leader-unitedlex-targets-rapid-expansion-after-acquisition-by-pe-heavyweight-cvc.

"25% of the Global Fortune 500": UnitedLex, "CVC Capital Partners Announces a Majority Interest Investment in UnitedLex," news release, September 20, 2018, unitedlex.com/news/ cvc-capital-partners-announces-majority-interest-investment.

"Elevate Services": Roy Strom, "Behind Elevate's Buying Binge," Law. com, February 7, 2019, law.com/americanlawyer/2019/02/07/ behind-elevates-buying-binge-liam-browns-meticulous-strategy.

"Mark Cohen of Legal Mosaic": Mark A. Cohen, "There Is Nothing 'Alternative' About New Model Providers–Especially the Big Four," *Legal Mosaic*, December 6, 2018, legalmosaic.com/there-is-nothing-alternative-about-new-model-providers-especially-the-big-four/.

"PwC earned $500 million": Nicholas Bruch and James Mayer, *Elephants in the Room: Part I — The Big Four's Expansion in the Legal Services Market* (ALM Intelligence, 2017), alm.com/intelligence/wp-content/ uploads/2017/09/NEW-VERSION-Elephants-in-the-Room-The-Big-4%E2%80%99s-Expansion-in-the-Legal-Services-Market-Final-9.15.17.pdf.

"20% of large law firms reported competing against the Big Four": Center on Ethics and the Legal Profession at Georgetown Law, Thomson Reuters Legal Executive Institute, Professional Service Firms (PSF) Group at Saïd Business School, University of Oxford, and Acritas, *Alternative Legal Service Providers 2019: Fast Growth, Expanding Use and Increasing Opportunity* (2019), legal.thomsonreuters.com/content/ dam/ewp-m/documents/legal/en/pdf/reports/alsp-report-final.pdf.

"increased insourcing by corporate legal departments": Rhys Dipshan, "Legal Departments Are Insourcing More Litigation Work Than Ever Before," Law.com, November 7, 2018, law.com/ legaltechnews/2018/11/07/legal-departments-are-insourcing-more-litigation-work-than-ever-before.

"It settled with the North Carolina State Bar": Daniel Fisher, "LegalZoom Settles Fight with North Carolina Bar Over Online Law," *Forbes*, October 22, 2015, forbes.com/sites/danielfisher/2015/10/22/legalzoom-settles-fight-with-north-carolina-bar-over-online-law/#3a6dcd643eb2.

"the company received a $500 million investment": Robert J. Ambrogi, "LegalZoom Zooms into $500 Million Secondary Investment," *LawSites*, July 31, 2018, lawsitesblog.com/2018/07/legalzoom-zooms-500-million-secondary-investment.html.

"John Suh, former CEO and now senior advisor at LegalZoom": Bill Carmody, "LegalZoom CEO Sees Quality Legal Advice as a Necessary Evil," *Inc.*, November 28, 2016, inc.com/bill-carmody/legalzoom-ceo-sees-quality-legal-advice-as-a-necessary-evil.html.

"they can sign up for an estate plan bundle": LegalZoom, "Estate Planning" (website), legalzoom.com/personal/estate-planning/get-your-estate-plan-today.html.

"LegalZoom's attorney-led trademark application package": LegalZoom, "Attorney-Led Trademark Registration" (website), legalzoom.com/business/intellectual-property/trademark-registration-overview-c.html.

"whether billing by the hour makes sense for modern clients": Zach Abramowitz, "Should Law Firms Still Use the Billable Hour?" *Above the Law*, July 11, 2017, abovethelaw.com/2017/07/should-law-firms-still-use-the-billable-hour.

"81% of corporate legal departments": Gartner, "Gartner Says 81 Percent of Legal Departments Are Unprepared for Digitalization," news release, December 12, 2018, gartner.com/en/newsroom/press-releases/2018-12-12-gartner-says-81-percent-of-legal-departments-are-unprepared-for-digitalization.

"the ABA's 2018 *TECHREPORT*": Ian Hu, "2018 Practice Management" in *TECHREPORT 2018* (ABA Legal Technology Resource Center, January 1, 2019), americanbar.org/groups/law_practice/publications/techreport/ABATECHREPORT2018/2018PracticeMgmt.

"ad costs are constantly on the rise": James Parsons, "Why Your Facebook Ads Keep Getting More Expensive," *Auto Likes*, November 16, 2018, autolikes.com/blog/2018/11/facebook-ads-getting-expensive.

"Facebook is still the world's largest social media network": J. Clement, "Most Famous Social Network Sites 2019, by Active Users," Statista, September 6, 2019, statista.com/statistics/272014/global-social-networks-ranked-by-number-of-users.

"Connie Brenton, former chair of the Corporate Legal Operations
Consortium": Roy Strom, "For Alternative Providers, Your Biggest
Client Is Their Biggest Opportunity," Law.com, November 14,
2017, law.com/corpcounsel/sites/americanlawyer/2017/11/14/for-
alternative-providers-your-biggest-client-is-their-biggest-opportunity.

"Gartner Hype Cycle": Gartner, "Gartner Hype Cycle," undated, gartner.
com/en/research/methodologies/gartner-hype-cycle.

"A study of 5,000 individuals over nearly 20 years": James H. Fowler and
Nicolas A. Christakis, "Dynamic Spread of Happiness in a Large Social
Network," *BMJ* (2008), doi.org/10.1136/bmj.a2338.

"lawyer and legal mindfulness expert Jeena Cho": Jeena Cho, "10 Things
They Don't Teach You in Law School (But Should)," Clio blog, updated
March 28, 2019, clio.com/blog/10-things-dont-teach-law-school.

CHAPTER 4

"the idea to 'surprise and delight' customers": Dan Gingiss, "4
Examples of Genuine 'Surprise and Delight' Moments to Try
in Your Business," *Forbes*, February 15, 2018, forbes.com/sites/
dangingiss/2018/02/15/4-examples-of-genuine-surprise-and-delight-
moments-to-try-in-your-business.

"a 76% increase in year-over-year revenue": Clio, "Palace Law: Increasing
Revenues by 76% with Clio as a Central Platform," undated, clio.com/
customers/palace-law-increasing-revenues-76-clio-central-platform

"*Good to Great*": Jim Collins, *Good to Great: Why Some Companies Make the
Leap... And Others Don't* (HarperBusiness, 2001).

"the main tenets of Amazon's flywheel": Gennaro Cuofano, "Amazon
Flywheel," FourWeekMBA, undated, fourweekmba.com/
amazon-flywheel.

"Amazon has always been customer-obsessed": Hoang Nam
Le, "Amazon Empire and Flywheel Effect (Part 1)," *FPT Tech
Insight*, October 25, 2018, techinsight.com.vn/language/en/
amazon-empire-and-flywheel-effect-part-1.

"over $230 billion in annual revenue": Macrotrends, "Amazon Revenue
2006-2019 | AMZN," accessed November 6, 2019, macrotrends.net/
stocks/charts/AMZN/amazon/revenue.

"33% share of the US ecommerce market": April Berthene, "Amazon
Grabs a Third of US Ecommerce Sales in 2018," *Digital Commerce
360*, February 27, 2019, digitalcommerce360.com/2019/02/27/
amazon-grabs-a-third-of-us-ecommerce-sales-in-2018.

"famed psychophysicist Howard Moskowitz": "Malcolm Gladwell: Do More Choices Make Us Happier?" interview by Guy Raz, TED *Radio Hour* from NPR, March 10, 2017, npr.org/templates/transcript/transcript.php?storyId=519265471.

"'People don't want to buy a quarter-inch drill'": Clayton M. Christensen, *The Clayton M. Christensen Reader* (Harvard Business Review, 2016).

"McDonald's wanted to sell more milkshakes": Clayton Christensen, "The 'Jobs to be Done' Theory of Innovation," in HBR *IdeaCast* from *Harvard Business Review*, interviewed by Amy Bernstein, podcast, 24:55, hbr.org/ideacast/2016/12/the-jobs-to-be-done-theory-of-innovation.

"Gerald suggested a few changes": "Marketing, Milkshakes and Understanding Your Customers," *Six Sigma Daily*, December 1, 2017, sixsigmadaily.com/marketing-milkshakes-understanding-your-customers.

CHAPTER 5

"Rule 7.4 of the ABA Model Rules of Professional Conduct": American Bar Association, "Rule 7.4: Communication of Fields of Practice & Specialization" in *Model Rules of Professional Conduct* online, updated October 30, 2019, americanbar.org/groups/professional_responsibility/publications/model_rules_of_professional_conduct/rule_7_4_communication_of_fields_of_practice_specialization.

"employees are encouraged to do whatever is needed": Roxanne Warren, "10 Things to Know About Zappos Customer Service," Zappos, August 30, 2018, zappos.com/about/customer-service-things-to-know

"when one woman called to return boots for her father": Micah Solomon, "Tony Hsieh Reveals the Secret to Zappos' Customer Service Success in One Word," *Forbes*, June 12, 2017, forbes.com/sites/micahsolomon/2017/06/12/tony-hsieh-spills-the-beans-the-one-word-secret-of-zappos-customer-service-success.

"Zappos being acquired by Amazon": "Amazon Closes Zappos Deal, Ends Up Paying $1.2 Billion," *Tech Crunch*, November 2, 2009, techcrunch.com/2009/11/02/amazon-closes-zappos-deal-ends-up-paying-1-2-billion.

"spending less on marketing": Natalie Zmuda, "Zappos Customer Service First — and a Daily Obsession," *AdAge*, October 17, 2008, adage.com/article/moy-2008/zappos/131759.

"the amazing internal culture": Susan M. Heathfield, "Find Out How
   Zappos Reinforces Its Company Culture," *The Balance Careers*, July 30,
   2019, thebalancecareers.com/zappos-company-culture-1918813.
"Starbucks says that its work is 'really about human connection' ":
   Starbucks, "Our Starbucks Mission Statement" (website), starbucks.
   ca/about-us/company-information/mission-statement.
"the store responded within 24 hours": Bob Thompson, "Starbucks
   Is Customer-Centric Because It Listened . . . to Me,"
   SocialMediaToday, April 17, 2012, socialmediatoday.com/content/
   starbucks-customer-centric-because-it-listened-me.
"offers them stock options": Samantha Sharf, "Why Starbucks Pays Its
   Baristas with Stock," Forbes, March 18, 2015, forbes.com/sites/
   samanthasharf/2015/03/18/why-starbucks-pays-its-baristas-with-
   stock-a-beginners-guide-to-company-stock.
"Birken Law": Birken Law (website), birkenlaw.com.

CHAPTER 6
"health psychologist and Stanford University lecturer Kelly McGonigal":
   Teresa Matich, "5 Tips to Manage Lawyer Stress—from Stress Expert
   Kelly McGonigal," Clio blog, October 30, 2019, clio.com/blog/
   lawyer-stress-kelly-mcgonigal.
"communication errors made up more than 40% of LAWPRO claims":
   LAWPRO, "Malpractice Claims Fact Sheets," undated, practicepro.ca/
   practice-aids/claims-fact-sheets.
"as Jeff Bezos famously does": John Koetsier, "Why Every Amazon
   Meeting Has at Least 1 Empty Chair," *Inc.*, April 5, 2018, inc.com/
   john-koetsier/why-every-amazon-meeting-has-at-least-one-empty-
   chair.html
"Ed Walters of Fastcase": Ed Walters, "Amazon LLP," on Medium.com,
   April 23, 2018, medium.com/@ejwalters/amazon-llp-1b721ed4baad.
"the subscription model": Teresa Matich, "How to Run a Subscription-
   Based Legal Practice," Clio blog, updated September 3, 2019, clio.
   com/blog/subscription-based-law-firm.
"the Solicitors Regulation Authority": Solicitors Regulation Authority,
   "Price Transparency," November 2018, sra.org.uk/solicitors/resources/
   transparency/transparency-price-service.
"*Mindset*": Carol Dweck, *Mindset* (Random House, 2006).

CHAPTER 7

"Cascade Legal Planning": Cascade Legal Planning, LLC (website), cascadelegalplanning.com.

"Estimated charges for various situations": Cascade Legal Planning, LLC, "Wills" (website), https://cascadelegalplanning.com/wills.

"His talk is available": Joshua Kubicki, "Business of Law Track: The Importance of the Client Journey," December 19, 2017, on Clio YouTube channel, video, 28:33, youtube.com/watch?v=HOc_qrTt_YM.

"five commonly used stages": Quick Sprout, "How to Create a Customer Journey Map that Converts," April 18, 2019, quicksprout.com/ customer-journey-map.

"customer journey map from Rail Europe": Neil Davey, "Nine Sample Customer Journey Maps — and What We Can Learn from Them," MyCustomer.com, July 30, 2018, mycustomer.com/experience/ engagement/nine-sample-customer-journey-maps-and-what-we-can-learn-from-them.

CHAPTER 9

"The word *empathy*": "Empathy (n.)," Online Etymology Dictionary, undated, etymonline.com/word/empathy.

"it wasn't until the mid-20th century": Susan Lanzoni, "A Short History of Empathy," *The Atlantic*, October 15, 2015, theatlantic.com/health/ archive/2015/10/a-short-history-of-empathy/409912.

"*The Future of the Professions*": Richard Susskind and Daniel Susskind, *The Future of the Professions* (Oxford University Press, 2016).

"Locks Law Firm": Clio, "How Moving to the Cloud Made Locks Law More Secure and Efficient," undated, clio.com/customers/ how-moving-to-the-cloud-made-locks-law-more-secure-and-efficient.

"Plain language is not just for legal writing": Cynthia Adams, " The Move Toward Using Plain Legal Language," *TYL*, undated, americanbar. org/groups/young_lawyers/publications/tyl/topics/writing/ the_move_toward_using_plain_legal_language.

"Katy Young of Ad Astra Law Group": Clio, "Helping Clients Through Hardships While Running a Profitable Firm," undated, clio.com/customers/ helping-clients-through-hardships-while-running-a-profitable-firm.

"the experience many clients face": Cat Moon (@inspiredcat),
    "#makeabetterlawyer #thread I needed a lawyer for a type of matter
    completely outside of my universe — for a people issue, not a business
    issue. People law. Not big law," Twitter, March 7, 2019, 2:18 p.m.,
    twitter.com/inspiredcat/status/1103736582631292929.

CHAPTER 10

"Embrace ambiguity": Patrice Martin, "Embrace Ambiguity," undated,
    Design Kit, video, 1:19, designkit.org/mindsets/5.

"five stages of the design thinking process": Hasso Plattner, *An Introduction
    to Design Thinking Process Guide* (Institute of Design at Stanford,
    undated), dschool-old.stanford.edu/sandbox/groups/designresources/
    wiki/36873/attachments/74b3d/ModeGuideBOOTCAMP2010L.pdf.

"Margaret Hagan": Margaret Hagan online portfolio (website),
    margarethagan.com

"*Law by Design*": Margaret Hagan, *Law by Design*, digital book, lawbydesign.
    co/en/home

"Cat Moon": Vanderbilt Law School, "Caitlin Moon," undated,
    law.vanderbilt.edu/bio/caitlin-moon.

"*The Toyota Way*": Jeffrey Liker, *The Toyota Way: 14 Management Principles
    from the World's Greatest Manufacturer* (McGraw-Hill Education,
    2004).

"collaborative brainstorming apps": "10 Collaborative Brainstorming
    Apps to Spark Your Team's Creativity," Gain blog, May 15, 2018, blog.
    gainapp.com/collaborative-brainstorming-apps-team-creativity.

"Designers can move forward and backward": Rikke Dam and Teo
    Siang, "Stage 2 in the Design Thinking Process: Define the
    Problem and Interpret the Results," Interaction Design Foundation,
    interaction-design.org/literature/article/stage-2-in-the-design-
    thinking-process-define-the-problem-and-interpret-the-results.

CHAPTER 11

"*Smart Collaboration*": Heidi K. Gardner, *Smart Collaboration* (Harvard
    Business Review Press, 2017).

"business strategist Heather Gray-Grant": Heather Gray-Grant,
    "Effectively Managing Change in a Law Firm," *Slaw*, May 22, 2018,
    slaw.ca/2018/05/22/effectively-managing-change-in-a-law-firm.

"your working memory": Jeffrey Dalto, "How to Chunk Training Materials," Convergence Training blog, October 31, 2014, convergencetraining. com/blog/chunk-training-materials.

CHAPTER 12

"there are 26 more who've remained silent": VHT, "Customer Service Stats That Matter: Part II," blog, undated, vhtcx.com/blog/ customer-service-stats-that-matter-part-ii.

"the completion rate drops by 5% to 20%": Brent Chudoba, "How Much Time Are Respondents Willing to Spend on Your Survey?" *Curiosity at Work* blog, SurveyMonkey, undated, surveymonkey.com/curiosity/ survey_completion_times.

"Billie Tarascio of Modern Law": Billie Tarascio, "Net Promoter Score in Law Firms," October 22, 2018, on Billie Tarascio YouTube channel, video, 10:29, youtube.com/watch?v=OoVEYuTgok4.

"Net Promoter Score": NICE Satmetrix, "What Is Net Promoter?" (website), netpromoter.com/know.

"NPS was introduced by marketing consultant Fred Reicheld": Frederick F. Reicheld, "The One Number You Need to Grow," *Harvard Business Review*, December 2003, hbr.org/2003/12/ the-one-number-you-need-to-grow.

"adopted by many companies": Net Promoter System, "Companies That Use Net Promoter" (website), netpromotersystem.com/about/ companies-using-nps.aspx.

"fair share of criticism": Jared M. Spool, "Net Promoter Score Considered Harmful (and What UX Professional Can Do About It)," UIE, December 20, 2017, articles.uie.com/net-promoter-score-considered- harmful-and-what-ux-professionals-can-do-about-it.

"Delighted": Delighted (website), delighted.com.

"CES was also introduced and popularized": Matthew Dixon, Karen Freeman, and Nicholas Toman, "Stop Trying to Delight Your Customers," *Harvard Business Review*, July-August 2010l, hbr. org/2010/07/stop-trying-to-delight-your-customers.

"Surveypal": Surveypal (website), surveypal.com.

"CSAT is calculated": Qualtrics, "What Is CSAT and How Do You Measure It?" (website), qualtrics.com/experience-management/customer/ what-is-csat.

"*Small Data*": Martin Lindstrom, *Small Data: The Tiny Clues That Uncover Huge Trends* (St. Martin's Press, 2016).

CONCLUSION

"Grand Bargain": Paul Lippe, "Will there be a 'New Deal'
for the legal profession?" Legal Rebels, *ABA Journal*,
October 21, 2015, abajournal.com/legalrebels/article/
will_there_be_a_new_deal_for_the_legal_profession.

"Ziva Law": Ziva Law (website), zivalaw.com.

JACK NEWTON has spearheaded efforts to educate the legal community on the security, ethics, and privacy issues surrounding cloud computing, and has become a nationally recognized writer and speaker on these topics. As the CEO and Co-founder of Clio and a pioneer in cloud-based legal technology, Jack also co-founded and is President of the Legal Cloud Computing Association (LCCA), a consortium of leading cloud computing providers with a mandate to help accelerate the adoption of cloud computing in the legal industry. He was also named a 2019 Fellow to the College of Law Practice Management, sits on the board of ROSS Intelligence, an AI-powered legal research provider, and is an investor in and advisor to early-stage legal tech startups.

🐦 @JACK_NEWTON

Legal Trends Report

By Clio

2019

79% of clients expect lawyers to respond within a day.

What else do clients expect from law firms?

Find out now at **clio.com/ltr**

Manufactured by Amazon.ca
Bolton, ON